James Gettys and the Founding of Gettysburg

Melissa Gettys; Amanda Howlett

authorHOUSE

AuthorHouse™
1663 Liberty Drive
Bloomington, IN 47403
www.authorhouse.com
Phone: 1 (800) 839-8640

Published by AuthorHouse 12/08/2016

ISBN: 978-1-5246-5335-4 (sc)
ISBN: 978-1-5246-5334-7 (e)

Print information available on the last page.

This book is printed on acid-free paper.

This book is dedicated to Uncle and Great Uncle Robert Gettys who forged the way with Gettys family research. Also to David D. Gettys, father and grandfather, for his positive support on this project.

Contents

PHOTO CREDITS

Photo 1   A modern photo of James Gettys' and Mary Gettys' grave memorial. Photo byAmanda Howlett.

Photo 2   A modern close-up photo of James Gettys' motif on the James Gettys andMary Gettys grave memorial. Photo by Amanda Howlett.

Photo 3   A modern photo of the gravestone of James' son Robert Todd Gettys, located behind his memorial. Photo by Amanda Howlett.

Photo 4   A modern photo of the memorial stone to James Gettys' nieces Sally Fleming and Isabella Ewing, located behind his memorial. Photo by Amanda Howlett.

Photo 5   Memorial marker for James Gettys' parents, Samuel and Isabella Gettys, in Black's Graveyard. Marker dedicated by William Gettys' family. Photo by Amanda Howlett.

Photo 6   A modern photo of the memorial plaque marking the original site of Gettys family homestead, located in Racehorse Alley. Photo by Amanda Howlett.

ACKNOWLEDGMENTS

IT GOES WITHOUT SAYING THAT no book can be written alone, even with two authors! The history of Gettysburg, Pennsylvania, and its people is vast, varying, and complex. There are many people whom we turned to for direction and clarification. Without assistance, the book would not be possible.

First and foremost, the authors are forever indebted to the Adams County Historical Society, from whence the truth be found: to Dr. Charles H. Glatfelter, who so graciously afforded us his opinions on new and crucial research findings; to Wayne Motts for his enthusiasm and support throughout the project; to Tim Smith and Randy Miller for help in locating documents; and to Larry Bolin for rerouting us when we felt we hit dead ends.

Secondly, the authors sincerely thank Mr. Jonathan Stayer, Head, Reference Section, Pennsylvania State Archives, for his in-depth knowledge and guidance through the records of the Pennsylvania Archives. In addition, we extend special thanks to the staff of the York County Archives, Borough of Gettysburg, and the Gettysburg Presbyterian Church for their assistance with original records. The authors thank the staff of the Adams County Library for their personal help with the very large number of books and resources used for this project. And, lastly, we extend a note of gratitude to the Evergreen Cemetery for the pristine upkeep of James Gettys' and his family's grave sites.

May the preservation of the past never cease!

CHAPTER ONE

Gettys Family Among Early Settlers

GENERAL JAMES GETTYS WAS BORN August 14, 1759, on his father's farm in the Marsh Creek Settlement, the area now known as Gettysburg. He was the fourth of eight children born to Samuel Gettys and Isabella Ramsey Gettys. He was born with a twin sister named Ann. While Ann's name was recorded in Martha Gettys Holland's family bible, it never appeared, again, thus intimating she died at birth.[1] James' other siblings included his older sisters Mary and Elizabeth, born 1752 and 1755, respectively, and one older brother, William, born in 1757. James' younger siblings included John, born 1761; Isabella, born 1764; and Martha, born 1768.[2]

Gettys family research conducted in the 1960s indicated a possibility of three older children belonging to Samuel: L.C Gettys, Alexander Gettys, and Samuel Gettys, Jr.[3] While two of those names appeared on the lottery map for the Gettysburg lots, they were not recorded as siblings in James' younger sister Martha's family Bible or in any wills or legal documents that James and his immediate family created. In addition, Samuel, Jr., was the given name of William's son, born 1779. Some confusion may lay there. An Alexander Gettys and another Samuel Gettys appeared on York County Taxables in 1783, in "Hamilton's Bann Township."[4] Alexander was listed as a single male with no property, and Samuel was listed as owning acreage, but

---

[1] Martha Gettys Holland Family Bible. *Courtesy of ACHS.*

[2] Ibid.

[3] W. Arthur Gettys, Descendant of James Gettys. Letter to author's grandfather, Harold Binkley Gettys. 23 May 1964.

[4] Egle, William Henry, Ed. Pennsylvania Historical & Museum Commission. "Provincial Papers: Returns of Taxables of the County of York, for the Years 1779, 1780, 1781, 1782 and 1783." *Pennsylvania Archives.* Harrisburg: State of Pennsylvania, 1897. 734; 280, 383, 601.

no animals. The connection between Alexander and James Gettys' family was unclear; however, as Alexander was never listed in any family documents, either, he was in the Gettys family, but not likely James' brother. In addition, the Samuel listed as owning acreage on the Hamilton's Bann tax list was, most likely, James' father, as Samuel bought and sold land in several townships at that time. With regards to a L.C. Gettys, no such person was traced. The Gettysburg map listed other Gettys, for example a C.D. Gettys; however, no L.C. appeared there or in any other family records. Again, as all these people appearing within the same few miles were most likely family; however, they were not James' siblings.

The Gettys family was of Scotch-Irish decent. The exact date of James' father, Samuel's arrival in Pennsylvania is unknown. Samuel Gettys' name appeared on the Agnew-McPherson List as having owned two tracts of land, originally, in 1740 and 1741: 1) near Rock Creek in May 1741 and 2) near Middle Creek in May 1740. It was difficult to determine the exact date of purchase. First, Samuel's proprietary papers were not recorded until April 10, 1765, in which part of the arrangement includes back rent on the land due from 1741.[5] If Samuel owed 24 years of back rent, that meant he was one of thousands of Pennsylvanians who dodged the provincial taxes. Living in what was considered the frontier, tax collection was rare. Secondly, it was likely that Samuel was in his twenties in 1740 or 1741, as during the American Revolution, he was included in a list of Associators, whose ages ranged between 16-60.[6] Thus, while there is no doubt that Samuel Gettys did own his property in the Marsh Creek

[5] State of Pennsylvania. Land Office. "Warrant - Samuel Gettys." 16 April 1865. Gettys File. *Courtesy of ACHS.*

[6] Pennsylvania Historical & Museum Commission. "Revolutionary War Records at the Pennsylvania State Archives: The Military Association, 1775-1777." *Pennsylvania State Archives.* 2011. Web. 21 Aug. 2011.; Egle, William H., Ed. Pennsylvania Historical & Museum Commission. "Pennsylvania in the War of the Revolution Associated Battalions and Militia of the Revolution 1775-1783." *Pennsylvania Archives.* Series 2, Vol. XIV. Harrisburg: State Printer, 1888. 454-468.

Settlement, it is difficult to prove that he was the original owner who purchased it in 1740.

Samuel Gettys and his wife Isabella Ramsey were of Scottish descent. James remained loyal to his heritage. His personal home library included four volumes of *the Scottish Register*, two volumes of Robert Burns' works, and a copy of *The Discarded Son*.[7] At that early date, there was one popular 4 volume work entitled *The Scottish Register*, a book that detailed the history of Scottish family tartans. The Burns volumes were, most likely, part of a 6 volume set of the 1806 publication of poems by Scottish born poet, Robert Burns. Significantly, Burns was actually born the same year as James Gettys, 1759. *The Discarded Son* was a Gothic tale written by popular Irish author Regina Maria Roche. Roche's murder mysteries were said to have had a wide male readership.

The families in the Marsh Creek Settlement did not default on their children's education. Reverend Alexander Dobbin opened his school in 1788 in what was and is still known as the Dobbin House. At that point, James Gettys was already 29, however. Thus, James and most of his contemporaries were more likely self-taught men. James continued educating himself throughout his adult life, as well. His library also included books on the laws of Pennsylvania and a collection of 96 British classics.[8]

In contrast to popular depiction, however, the children of the very early settlers did not spend all of their days in schoolhouses. Survival took precedent, and that meant hard work. Initially, life for the Gettys family in the Marsh Creek Settlement, now Adams County, was rewarding, yet rough. Purchasing land from the Penns did not necessarily mean it was guaranteed or free of squatters. Land tracts were large, and even with formal surveys, encroachment was common, albeit not usually intentional. James' father, Samuel, filed several caveats arguing bits and pieces of his farm were drawn into other men's surveys. Records from the Pennsylvania Land Office in 1765

---

[7] McClean, William Archibald, Ed. "General James Gettys, Proprietor." *Compiler Scrapbook*. Gettysburg: Compiler, 1908. 12. *Courtesy of* ACHS.

[8] Ibid. 12.

and 1768 already showed Samuel defending his property from other settlers, a history doomed to repeat itself.[9]

To the early settlers, winning a dispute over land ownership was worth the effort, especially west of the Susquehanna River. The land of rural Pennsylvania afforded settlers an abundance of natural resources. The families, however, worked hard to garner them. While east of the Susquehanna River was more barren, west of the river was dense with trees, both hardwoods and softwoods, for building everything from houses and barns to wagons and furniture. The types of wood included oak, hickory, chestnut, and pine.[10] Each family staked its claim to land; worked it; and built its home, upgrading as time, money, and resources allowed.

The work, however, was difficult, time consuming, and cumbersome. Settlers spread out, distancing themselves from one another, in order to grow crops to store for an entire year. That meant each family physically chopped down its own trees and took the wood to sawmills for processing or saved enough money and bought wood, directly. In addition, after the wood was processed, each family erected its own cabin, shelter, or shack, all with saws and tools that were still relatively primitive.

While movies and stories often depicted early settlers living in what were picturesque log cabins, this was not usually the case. The homes were often simple wooden frame houses, a basic design for survival from the elements. As families grew, these basic wooden shacks were replaced with larger, more elaborate log houses, but that took time, money, and resources. The smaller wood plank structures were not torn down, at first. The families used the smaller, older home structures for storage of foodstuffs, grain, and tools.[11] Early records

---

[9] Egle, William Henry. Pennsylvania Historical and Museum Commission. "Caveat Books 1748-1784." *Pennsylvania Archives*. Series 3, Vol. II, Harrisburg: Clarence M. Busch, State Printer, 1894. 329-30.

[10] *History of Cumberland and Adams Counties, Pennsylvania*. Chicago: Warner Beers, 1886. 53-4.Cited hereafter as *History of Cumberland and Adams Counties, Pennsylvania*.

[11] Ibid.61-2.

of Samuel Gettys' first log home intimate construction around 1769.[12] As James was born ten year earlier in 1759, he was most likely born in a small frame house, like most other settlers. Samuel built the larger, well known log home over time, after saving money and collecting all the needed resources.

Another major advantage afforded to settlers of the Adams County area was the availability of fresh, clean water from Marsh Creek, Rock Creek, and area springs, all originating at the base of the mountains. This engendered commerce, and the Marsh Creek area soon had several sawmills west of the Susquehanna River supporting the growing need for lumber. When Samuel Gettys built his log home, one such nearby sawmill was called McGack's, located on the Marsh Creek.[13]

The rich resources of the Pennsylvania waterways also supplied families with a steady diet of black bass, rock bass, and catfish. Wild duck and fowl were also abundant in and around the Marsh Creek and Rock Creek areas.[14] The Gettys family had plenty of meat available to them, which was an integral part of settlers' survival while they established their own farms and purchased farm animals of their own.

In fact, William Penn was so impressed with the abundance of wild animals in Pennsylvania that he included a description of them in a letter written in 1683 to the Committee of Free Society Traders, in hopes of attracting businessmen and traders to the province. He wrote there were plenty of animals for food, including "elk, as big a small ox; [and] deer, bigger than ours." In addition, Penn added there were birds and fowl, an abundance of pheasant, partridge, ducks,

---

[12] Glatfelter, Charles H. and Arthur Weaner. *The Settlers of the Manor of Maske Being the Documentary and Commentary for the Map: The Subdivision of the Manor of Maske.* Gettysburg: ACHS, 1989.; Glatfelter, Charles H. and Larry Bolin. Adams County Historical Society. *Manor of the Maske:11-21.* Gettysburg: ACHS, n.d., Cumberland Township Section, 2.

[13] York County Heritage Trust. *York County Heritage Trust Grant Voader Mill Collection.* York County Archives. n.d. Web. 29 January 2011. Cited hereafter as York County Heritage Trust. *York County Heritage Trust Grant Voader Mill Collection.*

[14] *History of Cumberland and Adams Counties, Pennsylvania.* 54.

geese, pigeons, and "turkeys (forty and fifty pounds weight) which is very good."[15]

While meat was an important component to survival, so were grains. Establishing a productive family farm was necessary for survival in rural Pennsylvania. Having the land, however, did not ensure success at farming. Growing enough grain to make bread entailed clearing land, planting seeds, waiting out the growing season, harvesting the wheat or corn, and taking it to a grist mill for grinding. As newcomers to this country, settlers like the Gettys family cleared their own farmland and experimented with seeds, finding the crops that worked for the soil and elements.

One of the most popular crops for settlers was corn. It was fairly reliable, and it fulfilled multiple needs, feeding not only humans but also their animal stock. Small amounts of corn was ground into meal using a tin grater. Large crops of corn or wheat, however, had to be transported to a grist mill for grinding, which entailed one day's travel time. Fortunately, by 1767, Cobean's Mill was open for business on the Marsh Creek.[16] The local grist mill afforded farmers choices. They could plant a wider variety of grains for special needs, in addition to their standard crops, as short trips to the mill were possible and not as costly and time consuming as one day's drive.

In addition to hard work, the Marsh Creek settlers had a strong sense of religion, which created a tight community and set guidelines for how the members functioned. The Gettys family attended the Upper Marsh Creek Presbyterian Church, which adhered to strict rules and held high moral values, particularly the Ten Commandments. In fact, members who acted in a manner not considered morally and religiously appropriate were banned from attending services, whilst the ruling members debated the

---

[15] Proud, Robert. *History of Pennsylvania 1681-1770*. Vol. I., 1797. Philadelphia: Poulson; Harrisburg: PA State Library, 1967. 246-50.

[16] York County Heritage Trust. *York County Heritage Trust Grant Voader Mill Collection*.

appropriate punishment.[17] Such strong convictions in God held the community together. The church members were bound by moral laws and reliant on each other to keep them. These values shaped young James and created a man who was sincere, benevolent, and trusted by the community.

Even early on, the small community looked after each other. In fact, in 1772 and 1773, James' father, Samuel, was appointed Overseer of the Poor for Cumberland Township.[18] In addition, Samuel held land in trust for the children of Adam Vance, a neighbor who passed away, abruptly in 1777, followed by his wife, shortly thereafter. While holding the land for the children, Samuel managed the farming and paid the taxes so that the Vance children had property of their own when they came of age.[19]

Not all of the families in the area struggled, however. The Vance family, for example, owned an extraordinary amount of land, animals, and personal belongings. Of the several Vance men in the area, John, Ezakial, Charles, and Adam, Adam was the most successful. Upon his death, his household inventory showed he had accrued a large amount of property, over 600 acres, which he successfully farmed. In addition, he owned a substantial amount of livestock: 2 bulls, 4 cows, 6 heifers, 12 steer, 2 oxen, and 12 horses. His wife owned petticoats, pocketbooks, and silk gowns, not the usual articles of clothing for the March Creek area settlers.[20] While Samuel Gettys' connection to the Vances remains unknown, it was through Samuel's

---

[17] "Church History: View of the Minutes-1777-78." Gettysburg Presbyterian Church. nd. Web. 30 May 2011.

[18] York County Archives. "December 8 1773." *Clerk of Courts Quarter Session Dockets 1749-1876.* York County, Pennsylvania. *York County Archives.* n.d. Web. 29 Jan. 2011.;York County Archives. "March 25 1772." *Clerk of Courts Quarter Session Dockets 1749-1876.* York County, Pennsylvania. *York County Archives.* n.d. Web. 29 Jan. 2011.

[19] Egle, William Henry, Ed. Pennsylvania Historical & Museum Commission. "Provincial Papers: Returns of Taxables of the County of York, for the Years 1779, 1780, 1781, 1782 and 1783." *Pennsylvania Archives.* Harrisburg: State of Pennsylvania, 1897. 734; 280, 383, 601.

[20] "Will of Adam Vance." *York County Archives.* June 2011 Pdf. June 2011.

generosity that the children of Adam Vance were able to begin life with the advantages justly belonging to them, through their family inheritance.

Ultimately, the survival and advancement of the Gettys family in the Marsh Creek Settlement was attributed to their hard work and faith, as well as the unity and resourcefulness of the town. Notwithstanding, James' father, Samuel Gettys, deserves credit for not only his rugged bravery, but also his ability to provide for a wife and his seven children, as well as the four orphaned children of a friend. Keeping a large family in food, wood, and woolens, took a lot of land, patience, and money. Thus to purchase all the large family needed for survival, James' father opened what became a landmark in Pennsylvania, the Gettys Tavern.

CHAPTER TWO

Gettys Tavern and the American Revolution

IN 1761, WHEN JAMES GETTYS was two years old, his father, Samuel, opened the Gettys Tavern. Growing up in his father's prominent tavern, James had a childhood filled with social interaction. Taverns were more than just a location for drinking and lodging. They were significant meeting places for area residents. Farms were far apart, and such interactions helped communities keep pace with news and trade. The Gettys Tavern also served as the local store, where basic goods were purchased and exchanged, such as loaf sugar, rice, and ribbon. Area residents preferred coffee to tea, and rum to ale. Accounts were kept, in ledger format. Few customers paid their entire bill in cash.[21] Thus, James grew up helping in the family business, "doing sums;" interacting with the people of the community; and learning the news from Philadelphia and Baltimore, first hand, from traveling customers. Such experiences bolstered his social and business skills and established him as a person of knowledge and trustworthiness, all at a relatively young age.

Whilst the tavern became an important meeting place for the Pennsylvania Rifle Battalion and militia during the American Revolution, it was not so aptly admired by the King of England's magistrates. In October of 1761, Samuel was arrested and charged with running a "Tippling House," or a house where liquor was sold and drank, in violation of the law.[22] James' father pleaded his case before the King's Court and was released, presumably after paying

---

[21] Miscellaneous purchase receipts of Samuel Gettys and Williams McPherson. c. 1786-7. Gettys File. *Courtesy of* ACHS.

[22] York County Archives. "October 1761." *Clerk of Courts Quarter Session Dockets 1749-1876.* York County, Pennsylvania. *York County Archives.* n.d. Web. 29 Jan. 2011.

for a license and settling any fines and taxes the British King's Court imposed. Forthwith, the Gettys Tavern remained a legal establishment, as James' father dutifully renewed his tavern license each July from 1762 until 1789, the year before he died.[23]

In the eighteenth century, tavern owners or "landlords" were well respected men. In fact, when Samuel first opened the tavern, licensees were required to put up a bond, and the bond was guaranteed by a member of the community who attested to the fact that the licensee was an upstanding member. Each year Samuel applied for a license, citizens in the community attested to his honor and character, and posted the bond required by law.[24] As tavern owners, the Gettys family had a reputation of propriety and respectability during the tenure of the establishment.

In addition for being bonded, landlords obeyed the curfew laws restricting drinking hours. They turned patrons out each evening by 9:00 o'clock. On the Sabbath day, the doors remained locked until after the conclusion of local church services.[25] Even the community, itself, depended on the tavern keeper or "landlord." As the town tavern also served as a public meeting house; a supply store; and a distribution center for news, goods, and mail carried in by travelers, the tavern was the hub of every town. Popular and well-renowned, the Gettys Tavern was no exception.

By the early 1770s, public discussions and debate in public houses included its share of anti-British sentiment. Whether citizens were loyalists, rebels, or somewhere in-between, people's conversations centered on the effect of British policies on the American colonies. In response to the need for organized discussion among the colonies, individual counties elected their own committees of communication. Representatives were responsible for maintaining communication

---

[23] Ibid. There are 23 additional licenses for Samuel Gettys beginning July 1762 and ending July 1789.

[24] York County Archives. "July 29, 1763." *Clerk of Courts Quarter Session Dockets 1749-1876*. York County, Pennsylvania. *York County Archives*. n.d. Web. 29 Jan. 2011.

[25] Earle, Alice Morse. *Stage Coach and Tavern Days*. New York: Macmillan, 1915. 35.

with like committees in the other colonies. On July 4, 1774, York County, which included modern day Adams County, held an election for the formation of such a committee. Archibald McClean, a local surveyor and trusted businessman, was elected the committeeman from the area. The committee met on December 16, 1774, in York, Pennsylvania, to discuss and disseminate information put forth by the Continental Congress in Philadelphia.[26] Thus, the citizens of the county now had an official committee member and representative.

In January, 1775, the British troops began an aggressive front against anti-British protests and gatherings. As the Massachusetts colonists fought back, the King declared the colonies in rebellion and halted trade to America. The second Continental Congress convened, calling on all colonies to send forth volunteers for service in the Continental Army. The message was dispersed through the committees of communication. Answering the call of the Continental Congress, men from the Marsh Creek Settlement and the surrounding territories met at Samuel Gettys' Tavern on June 24, 1775, and formed a militia unit. The unit went to York and joined with the regiment of Captain Michael Doudle. By the end of July, 1775, the Pennsylvania Rifle Battalion, 1st Pennsylvania Regiment, Company C, was engaged in active duty in Massachusetts.[27]

In addition, each colony was told to organize its own militia. On June 30, 1775, the Commonwealth approved an "Association entered into by the good People of this province for the Defense of their Lives, Liberty and Property."[28] The Associations were formed by county and led by a Committee of Safety, which included such prominent Pennsylvania names as Benjamin Franklin and John Dickinson, and such prominent area men as Michael Swoope. These

---

[26] *History of Cumberland and Adams Counties, Pennsylvania.* .32-3.

[27] Linn, John Blair and William H. Egle, eds. Pennsylvania Historical and Museum Commission. "Colonel William Thompson's Battalion of June 25, 1775-July 1, 1776."*Pennsylvania Archives.* Series 2, Vol. X. Harrisburg: Edwin K. Meyers, State Printer, 1891. 20.

[28] Hoban, Charles F., Ed. Pennsylvania Historical and Museum Commission. "Votes of Assembly 1775." Pennsylvania Archives. Series 8, Vol. VIII. January 7, 1771-September 26, 1776. Harrisburg: State of Pennsylvania, 1935. 7245.

men were responsible for calling the Associators or militia into action, as needed.[29] Each county was mandated to supply the "proper Number of good new Firelocks, with Bayonets fitted to them, cartridge Boxes, and Twenty-three Rounds of Cartridge . . . and Knapsacks." York County was required to supply 300 of each and to "select a number of Minute-Men, equal to the Arms &c provided for the same, to be in Readiness, upon the shortest Notice, to march to any Quarter in Case of Emergency."[30] Though not always a well known fact, Pennsylvania had its own Minute-Men, too. By February of 1776, the number of British troops had multiplied, forcing Pennsylvania's Assembly to officially form armed units for the protection of the Commonwealth and contribution to General Washington's Continental Army. These troops were formed from the best marksmen in Pennsylvania and called the Pennsylvania Riflemen. This is where James Gettys began his official service to the Commonwealth and the Country

In addition to the mandate for militia, the Commonwealth set forth resolutions fining any "Male white Person, capable of bearing Arms, between the Ages of Sixteen and Fifty years" who refused to join the Association and drill with the militia. Such men were termed Non-Associators. State Assessors of townships, boroughs, wards, and districts were required to "go to the Place or Places of Abode of all and every Person and persons" and ascertain who was capable of bearing arms. Any Assessor who refused to submit a list to the Commonwealth was fined a hefty amount: 10 pounds.[31] Thus, the Commonwealth's Assessors literally took to the streets.

In order to locate most of the populace, the Assessors chose gathering locations convenient for most of the area men. The locations were public meeting rooms or appropriate and centrally located public venues. The Gettys Tavern was the site chosen for recording names of local non-associators and collecting their fines of 3 pounds 10 shillings,

---

[29] Ibid. 7247, 7246.
[30] Ibid.
[31] Ibid. 7380-1.

per person.[32] On June 9, 1777, the area Assessors recorded the names of men whom they fined. Two hundred and fourteen "non-associators" from the area townships were ordered to appear at the Gettys Tavern to pay their fines: 19 from Strabann;" 41 from "Hamilton Bawn;" 11 from "Mt. Joy;" and 143 from "Cumberland."[33]

This procedure was not very popular among some citizens of the Commonwealth, and usually for very legitimate reasons. Some farms were just too large and far away for traveling back and forth to drill. In addition, some settlers were simply too poor and ill equipped to come ready supplied with weapons, ammunition, and food for the duration. These families were given a chance to voice their concerns at meetings held, again, at public venues and with the Assessors.[34] This style of open dialogue between the Commonwealth and its people continued well into the future, as a posting appeared in the Carlisle Gazette in 1789, calling meetings for those "aggrieved by fines imposed for neglect of military duty" scheduled at several homes in the area, one being "the house of Samuel Gettys, in Gettysburgh."[35] Likewise, the "house of Samuel Gettys," James' father, was the official meeting place for property tax assessors hearing appeals. One such reference was written directly on the tax list of 1786: "But if any think themselves aggrieved . . . the day of appeal is the 29th Day of May at the house of Samuel Gettys."[36] Thus, James Gettys learned his civic duties directly from his father, Samuel.

---

[32] Young, Henry James. *York County, Pennsylvania, in the American Revolution: A Source Book.* Gettysburg: ACHS, 1935. 199.

[33] Ibid. 210-212, 231.

[34] Hoban, Charles F., Ed. Pennsylvania Historical and Museum Commission. "Votes of Assembly 1775." Pennsylvania Archives. Series 8, Vol. VIII. January 7, 1771-September 26, 1776. Harrisburg: State of Pennsylvania, 1935. 7383.

[35] "Pennsylvania Herald and York General Advertiser: Sept 2 1789." *Abstracts of South Central Pennsylvania newspapers 1785-1790* Westminster: Family Line, P., 1988. 118. Courtesy of ACHS.

[36] York County, PA Board of County Commissioners. "Cumberland Township." *Tax Records Franklin, Monaghan, Warrington, Dover, Newberry, Manchester, Mount Joy, Huntingdon, Straban, Cumberland, Hamilton Bann, and Reading Twps, 1786.* (1). Microfilm. Roll 5222.

It was during this time period, that history began recording some public meetings in Samuel Gettys' establishment as meetings in his "home," not always his "tavern." The Gettys' family business evolved, meeting a broader range of needs in the community. The meetings were significant, as were the crowds. It is likely that the original tavern built prior to 1761 was either modified or abandoned, and the new establishment was the larger, more accommodating log building commonly referred to as the Gettys family home. This building was larger than a small tavern, thus it could have housed the tavern, store, and family residence.

The Gettys family and the Gettys Tavern also played an ongoing role during the American Revolution. The tavern functioned as the local exchange and supply store and became the center of distribution of food, grain, and goods for the area residents as well as the Continental Army. Large farmers and suppliers such as the Gettys were of utmost importance to the Army and the community after the British-imposed freeze on trade. Goods were scarce and food hard to come by, hence, the prices inflated. Farmers and shopkeepers struggled collecting debt owed them, let alone providing food and goods to the armed forces on account or receipt. Yet, once again, the Gettys family stood in support of the colonies. In 1780, William Scott, the purchasing commissioner for the York County area, submitted receipts of goods received from Samuel Gettys for use by the Continental Army. Purchases were recorded as 90 pounds for 3 tons of flour on January 15, 1780; 30 pounds for 1 ton of flour on January 30, 1780; and 12 pounds 10 shillings for 100 bushels of oats on January 30, 1780.[37] Such a quantity of grains did not come from the Gettys farm, alone. Samuel acted on behalf of the community as the coordinator and distributor of food and supplies in support of the Revolutionary cause.

Likewise, Pennsylvanians were responsible for feeding the Pennsylvania Associators or militia men during the Revolutionary War. Although the state commissioners purchased the goods during the war, many times the Commonwealth paid the farmers

---

[37] Young, Henry James et al. *York County, Pennsylvania, in the American Revolution.* Red Series. Vol. III. 569. Gettysburg: ACHS, 1958.

and shopkeepers much later, if at all. Receipts were approved by the Governor before payment was made, which took organization and money. With the country at war, each colony was responsible for feeding its own militia. Again, Samuel Gettys offered food and supplies in support of the cause. One such receipt appeared in the submission of extended debt owed to shopkeepers by the State of Pennsylvania for supplies given the militia during the war. One receipt, dated Friday, June 24, 1791, read, "The following accounts settled by the comptroller and Register General - were this day approved by the Governor."[38] Here, Samuel Gettys, again, appeared as a supplier of the soldiers: "Of Samuel Gettys for two blankets furnished to a detachment of Militia of this state, and for victualing the said Militia in 1776 amounting to seven pounds sixteen shillings and six pence."[39] Unfortunately, by the time the receipt was approved for payment, Samuel was deceased.

James' father, Samuel, passed away on what was recorded Monday, March 5, 1790. March the 5th was not a Monday, on the common calendar, that year. Perhaps there was confusion or a misprint. In his obituary, Samuel was listed as shopkeeper, not tavern owner, emphasizing the significance of the establishment to the war and the town. A healthy man until the end, Samuel fell ill only hours prior to his death.[40] When Samuel died, so did the famed Gettys Tavern.

After his father's death, James did not apply for a tavern license until 1798, 8 years later. He obtained his liquor license and served liquor in his own new establishment on York Street in 1798 and 1799.[41] The building was a modest, two story brick building, 42' x 36', with 5

---

[38] MacKinney, Gertrude, Ed. Pennsylvania Historical and Museum Commission. "Executive Minutes of Governor Thomas Mifflin 1790-1792." *Pennsylvania Archives*. Series 9, Vol. I, Harrisburg: State of PA, 1931. 140-141.

[39] Ibid. 144.

[40] "*YORK, March 24, 1790.*" *Pennsylvania Herald and York General Advertiser.* Gettys File. *Courtesy of* ACHS.

[41] York County Archives. "September Sessions 1798." *Clerk of Courts Quarter Session Dockets 1749-1876. York County Archives.* n.d. Web. 29 Jan. 2011. ; York County Archives. "June Sessions 1799." *Clerk of Courts Quarter Session Dockets 1749-1876. York County Archives.* n.d. Web. 29 Jan. 2011.

windows.[42] By 1800, the establishment was more of an inn, hosting meetings and events for the local community. On such newspaper notice for a meeting held in the building referred to James Gettys as the "Innkeeper."[43] In the years that followed, the tavern part of the building was actively run by tenants who leased out the taproom. One advertisement for a tenant appeared in the February 13, 1805, edition of the *Centinel*: : "To be Let, For a Term of Years, That well known TAVERN SEAT, in the town of Gettysburg, Adams County."[44] The building was listed "of brick" and "two stories high" with "two front lots of ground," matching the description of his inn and residence.[45] It was unclear whether James and his young family kept their residence in the inn or with his mother, Isabella, in his father's log home. James owned both buildings until 1810.[46]

---

[42] York County, Pennsylvania, Board of County Commissioners. "Cumberland Township 1799." *York County Tax Records 1799*.York County Archives. n.d. Microfilm. 6 June 2011. Roll #5227.

[43] Wright, F. Edward, Comp. "York Recorder: Nov. 4 1800." *Abstracts of South Central Pennsylvania Newspapers 1796-1800*. Westminster: Family Line P., 1988. 122. Courtesy of ACHS.

[44] Gettys, James. Advertisement. *Gettysburg:Centinel, February 13, 1805*. Gettys File. *Courtesy of ACHS*.

[45] Ibid.

[46] Borough of Gettysburg. *Gettysburg Minute Book 1806-1840*. Gettysburg: Borough of Gettysburg, 1806-1840. 39-45, 4.

CHAPTER THREE

Military Career and Military Family

JAMES' MILITARY CAREER OFFICIALLY BEGIN in 1776 when General Washington requested additional troops to serve in the Continental Army. Recognizing Washington's need, and that of the Commonwealth, on February 20, 1776, the House put forth a Resolution to raise an additional 2000 troops to be termed the Pennsylvania Riflemen. These unique troops were divided into two smaller battalions of 1000 men, each, and called into active duty, immediately. Hence, on June 30, 1776 James Gettys joined Captain Philip Albright's Company as a Sergeant, First Battalion, and immediately marched to New York to join General Washington's Continental Army.[47] On August 27, upon arrival in New York, Captain Albright's Company took part in one of the first major battles of the American Revolutionary War, the Battle of Brooklyn.[48]

Literally surrounded on the island of Brooklyn, General Washington's troops took an enormous loss, including a large number of men taken prisoner and missing in action. Unfamiliar with their surroundings and cut off on all sides, men scrambled to return to the mainland, only to drown in deep water or be cut down by the Hessian

---

[47] Linn, John Blair and William H. Egle, eds. Pennsylvania Historical and Museum Commission. "Pennsylvania in the War of the Revolution, Battalions and Line. 1775-1783. Volume I: Pennsylvania Rifle regiment, Col. Miles." *Pennsylvania Archives.* Series 2, Vol. X. Harrisburg: Edwin K. Meyers, State Printer, 1891. 201-2, 217-18. Gettys, Melissa and Amanda Howlett. "The Military Career of James Gettys." *Adams County History.* ACHS, 2017.

[48] Linn, John Blair and William H. Egle, eds. Pennsylvania Historical and Museum Commission. "Pennsylvania in the War of the Revolution, Battalions and Line. 1775-1783. Volume I: Pennsylvania Rifle regiment, Col. Miles." *Pennsylvania Archives.* Series 2, Vol. X. Harrisburg: Edwin K. Meyers, State Printer, 1891. 202, 206. Gettys, Melissa and Amanda Howlett. "The Military Career of James Gettys." *Adams County History.* ACHS, 2017.

soldiers fighting for the British. On an official roll of the missing, wounded and dead troops taken on September 1st, 1776, James Gettys was recorded as "Mising since Battle."[49] Other area men missing and captured in the battle included William McPherson, Thomas Foster, and Charles Spangler.

Lists of prisoners and exchanged prisoners are rare and far from all inclusive. A partial list of officers from a prisoner exchanged on April 20th, 1778, included several men from James Gettys' local unit, including life long friend William McPherson. It is likely James was part of that prisoner exchange.[50]

James Gettys' military career continued as he volunteered, once again, in 1781 for a Light Horse and Volunteer Company, a unit under the command of friend and Captain William McPherson. James was assigned the position of Cornet, a lower ranking officer position. Eager to assist their fellow countrymen, the unit was described as "spirited" by Brigadier General James Irvine in a report to Council on August 18, 1781.[51]

The Revolutionary War Military Card File system lists James Gettys' second unit as Non-Active, meaning they were organized, drilled, and awaited orders; however, they were not called into active

[49] Linn, John Blair and William H. Egle, eds. Pennsylvania Historical and Museum Commission. "Pennsylvania in the War of the Revolution, Battalions and Line. 1775-1783. Volume I: Pennsylvania Rifle regiment, Col. Miles." *Pennsylvania Archives.* Series 2, Vol. X. Harrisburg: Edwin K. Meyers, State Printer, 1891. 214-19. Gettys, Melissa and Amanda Howlett. "The Military Career of James Gettys." *Adams County History.* ACHS, 2017.

[50] Linn, John Blair and William H. Egle, eds. Pennsylvania Historical and Museum Commission. "Pennsylvania in the War of the Revolution, Battalions and Line. 1775-1783. Volume I: Pennsylvania Rifle regiment, Col. Miles." *Pennsylvania Archives.* Series 2, Vol. X. Harrisburg: Edwin K. Meyers, State Printer, 1891. 216-217. Gettys, Melissa and Amanda Howlett. "The Military Career of James Gettys." *Adams County History.* ACHS, 2017.

[51] *History of Cumberland and Adams Counties, Pennsylvania.* 34-5.; Pennsylvania Historical & Museum Commission. "Revolutionary War Military Abstract Card File: Items Between Gabell, Thomas and Gaddis, Joseph." *Military Accounts: Militia. Pennsylvania Archives.* Web. ARIAS: Pennsylvania Digital State Archives. "Military Accounts: Militia."

service.[52] James continued taking his military commitment seriously, and very soon, rose in rank. Following the culmination of the war, his name appeared in a letter written August 18, 1786, from William Scott to Benjamin Franklin, Esquire, presenting the "arrangement of York County Militia May, 1786." At that point, James was a Lieutenant under the command of Captain James Hamilton in a Troop of Light Horse. In ending the letter, Scott graciously addressed Benjamin Franklin in saying, "I am sir, Your Excellency's Most Obedient Humble Servant."[53] While the closing was fairly common, "Your Most Obedient Humble Servant," the addition of "I am Sir, your Excellency's Most Obedient and Humble Servant" was a reflection of the admiration held for Benjamin Franklin by area men, at that time.

James continued advancing in rank, as he appeared in the muster roll of the Pennsylvania Militia from 1790-1800 as a 2nd Major in the 4th Regiment.[54] By 1802, James held the position of Lieutenant Colonel of the 20th Regiment.[55] The militia played a similar roll to our modern day reserves, albeit mandatory. The men maintained their jobs and homes, drilled, and stepped into action when called.

Ascending to a higher rank had its downfalls, however, even for the founder of Gettysburg. In 1800, the political climate in Pennsylvania was highly charged, with loyalties mixed between Federalists and Democratic-Republicans. James Gettys was a Colonel at the time. Like his father before him, James held the militia meetings at his home. During one such meeting, debate ensued over Governor

---

[52] Pennsylvania Historical & Museum Commission. "Revolutionary War Military Abstract Card File: Items Between Gabell, Thomas and Gaddis, Joseph." *Military Accounts: Militia. Pennsylvania Archives.* Web. ARIAS: Pennsylvania Digital State Archives. "Military Accounts: Militia."

[53] Montgomery, Thomas Lynch, ed. Pennsylvania Historical & Museum Commission. "Militia Rolls." *Pennsylvania Archives.* Series 6, Vol. III. Harrisburg: State Printer, 1907. 1457.

[54] Montgomery, Thomas Lynch, Ed. Pennsylvania Historical & Museum Commission. "York County Militia 1790-1800." *Pennsylvania Archives.* Series 6, Vol. V. Harrisburg: State of PA, 1907. 831.

[55] MacKinney, Gertrude, Ed. Pennsylvania Historical & Museum Commission. "Executive Minutes of Governor Thomas McKean 1799-1808." *Pennsylvania Archives.* Series 9, Vol. III. Harrisburg: State of Pennsylvania, 1931. 1880-1881.

McKean's newly passed law requiring that the militia men changed their cockades, the ribbon on their uniform hats, from the traditional black to blue and red.[56] Many of the area militia officers, Federalists in political belief, felt that the Governor did not have the authority to change the traditional uniform. They felt he was overexerting his power, intentionally, showing the dominance of his Democratic-Republican Party.

Never-the-less, the officers replaced the black cockade with a blue and red one made from worsted wool ribbon. As James Gettys later attested, it was ribbon that was available in the stores, at that time. In addition, Gettys and his men tried creating a new cockade on short notice that was, as he said, the "same size as the Republicans."[57] However, Captain Alexander Cobean, a man very dedicated to his community and adamant in his Federal beliefs, refused to change the new cockade. In protest of the abrupt change in uniform by the new Governor, he continued wearing the traditional black cockade, as did several of his men.[58]

The militia's physician was Dr. William Crawford, an outspoken Democratic-Republican at the time. Dr. Crawford, known for his boisterous editorials in the daily newspaper, felt the area Federalists were not in compliance and accused them of breaking the "law." He complained to Colonel Kuhn (of New Oxford) that the ribbon the Federalists used did not warrant a proper cockade. He was also outraged that Captain Alexander Cobean's group did not switch cockades, immediately. Colonel Kuhn spoke with Colonel Gettys and told Dr. Crawford the issue was closed. The controversy subsided, for a while. However, a short time afterward in a parade through the streets of Gettysburg, Captain Alexander Cobean's men arrived and rode through the streets, still sporting traditional black cockades. In addition, Colonel James Gettys and his fellow officers still wore

---

[56] Ibid. 1673.

[57] Pennsylvania Department of State. "Republica vs Capt. Alexander Cobean." *Pennsylvania Archives*. Record Group: Dept. of State. Subgroup: Secty of Commonwealth. Series: Court Martial Proceedings. RG 26.4-0460. Box #1. 1790-March 1814.

[58] Ibid.

their blue and red worsted wool cockades. Disagreement ensued on what constituted propriety, causing a scuffle. The scuffle did not go unnoticed. The new commanding officer, Brigadier General Michael Simpson, filed charges against Colonel Gettys and his officers in the military court.[59]

The charges against Colonel James Gettys were filed on November 15, 1802. The court proceedings convened at the home of Major William Sturgeon in New Oxford, on December 6 of the same year. The case was titled "Republica[ns] versus James Gettys," clearly indicating any lack of inquiry or neutrality. The only two witnesses, both Democratic-Republicans, testified that Colonel Gettys seemed oblivious to the fact that Captain Cobean's unit refused to change cockades. Colonel Gettys, himself, objected, saying that the trial statements of the two witnesses were pre-arranged and given before "qualified." His desire to speak was stunted. No other witnesses were allowed, and the court stated he was guilty of allowing his men to train without what the law considered proper blue and red cockades. He was fined $10.00 and temporarily suspended from the position of Colonel.[60] Governor McKean issued a statement that he agreed with the findings as the "law cannot be dispensed with."[61] Ironically, ten months later, McKean was obligated to announce the results of an Adams County election, overwhelmingly electing James Gettys as sheriff!

All in all, sixteen other men were charged with wearing improper cockades. The men who pleaded guilty were issued small fines. The men who pleaded not guilty before the court were issued larger

---

[59] Ibid.; Pennsylvania Department of State. "Republica vs Col. James Gettys." *Pennsylvania Archives*. Record Group: Dept. of State. Subgroup: Secty of Commonwealth. Series: Court Martial Proceedings. RG 26.4-0460. Box #1. 1790-March 1814.

[60] Pennsylvania Department of State. "Republica vs Col. James Gettys." *Pennsylvania Archives*. Record Group: Dept. of State. Subgroup: Secty of Commonwealth. Series: Court Martial Proceedings. RG 26.4-0460. Box #1. 1790-March 1814.

[61] MacKinney, Gertrude, Ed. Pennsylvania Historical & Museum Commission. "Executive Minutes of Governor Thomas McKean 1799-1808." *Pennsylvania Archives*. Series 9, Vol. III. Harrisburg: State of Pennsylvania, 1931. 1880-1881.

fines and temporarily demoted. Among the men tried were other prominent Adams County Federalists: Captain Alexander Cobean, who later founded the Bank of Gettysburg and marched his men to the Port of Baltimore in the War of 1812; and Captain James Scott, the first Postmaster of Adams County. In addition, Lieutenant Colonel James Horner, Lieutenant James Wilson, Lieutenant Robert Hays, and Cornet John Foster were charged, tried, and fined. The man who officially filed the charges, Brigadier General Simpson, soon retired. Ironically, James Gettys was named Brigadier General, 5th Division, just prior to the War of 1812.[62]

Shocking as the thought of a court martial may be now, it was commonplace in the 19th century. The culture was different, and the concept of arguing a point in court was quite common, both on the civil and military levels. Even Paul Revere was court martialed. It was a manner of handling disagreements and discipline. Disgrace was more subjective and varied with one's loyalties and viewpoints.

By the War of 1812, the country's parties were no closer to agreement. However, the concept of another war with the British was not welcomed by either party, let alone all the citizens. Never-the-less, loyalty to the country prevailed, especially with the militia of Adams County. Governor Simon Snyder called for the preparation and organization of the militia on June 3, 1812, on orders from the Federal Government. President Madison declared war approximately 2 weeks following the organization of the country's militia.[63] Governor Simon Snyder named

---

[62] Pennsylvania Historical & Museum Commission. "Muster Rolls - Pennsylvania Militia War 1812-1814: With Contemporary Papers and Documents." *Pennsylvania Archives*. Series 2, Vol. XII. Harrisburg: E.K. Myers, State Printer, 1890.

[63] Bloom, Robert L. *A History of Adams County, Pennsylvania 1700-1990*. Gettysburg: ACHS, 1992.91.

James Gettys the Brigadier General of the 5th Division.[64] During the reorganization of the Pennsylvania Militia in 1814, Jacob Eyster was named Brigadier General and James Gettys became Vice.[65] As several area units took part in defending the Port of Baltimore in the War of 1812, these men played vital roles in maintaining the organization of the troops and keeping up morale for a war that few Americans wanted.

James was not the only Gettys active in the military. James' older brother, William, also had a well established military career. Muster rolls from the Revolutionary War showed two men named William Gettys from Pennsylvania. The William Gettys from York County was in the 10th Pennsylvania Regiment. The 10th Regiment marched out of York and fought in the Continental Army. William Gettys maintained active duty status for several years in duration. His records indicated active duty from January 1, 1777-August 1, 1780.[66] He appeared on the muster roll of Captain Jacob Weaver under the command of Colonel Richard Hampton in April, 1780.[67]

Following the war, William Gettys returned home to the Marsh Creek area and to his wife, Agnes Carson Gettys. William and Agnes followed her family in a move to Rutherford, North Carolina, where

---

[64] MacKinney, Gertrude, Ed. Pennsylvania Historical & Museum Commission. "Executive Minutes of Governor Thomas McKean 1799-1808." *Pennsylvania Archives*. Series 9, Vol. III. Harrisburg: State of Pennsylvania, 1931. 1880-1881. Pennsylvania Historical & Museum Commission. "Muster Rolls - Pennsylvania Militia War 1812-1814: With Contemporary Papers and Documents." *Pennsylvania Archives*. Series 2, Vol. XII. Harrisburg: E.K. Myers, State Printer, 1890. 3-4.

[65] Montgomery, Thomas Lynch, Ed. Pennsylvania Historical & Museum Commission. "War 1812=1814." *Pennsylvania Archives*. Series 6, Vol. VII. Harrisburg: Harrisburg P. Co., State Printer, 1907. 4.

[66] Pennsylvania Historical and Museum Commission. "Revolutionary War Military Abstract Card File: Items Between Gerum, Thos., and Geyer, Casper. Item 56." *Pennsylvania Digital State Archives*. n.d. Web. Feb. 2011.

[67] Montgomery, Thomas Lynch, Ed. Pennsylvania Historical and Museum Commission. "Continental Line, 10th Pennsylvania October 25, 1776-January 17, 1781." *Pennsylvania Archives*. Series 5, Vol. III. Harrisburg: Harrisburg P. Co., State Printer, 1906. 544.

they purchased a farm in Rutherford County.[68] Family records confirm that was the William Gettys mentioned above.

Records on James' younger brother John, however, remain questionable. According to family dates, John Gettys was just 16 years old when the Pennsylvania Congress passed the Act of Assembly requiring all men 16 - 50 take part in the militia or the group of "associators," preparing for service in the Revolutionary War. It was unknown whether John Gettys fought in the war; however, he was not listed as a non-associator. In addition, there was a "John Getty" listed with a York County Militia Battalion, enrolling on September 11, 1776.[69] That John Gettys attended Flying Camp and was assigned to the Marines.[70] In the Revolutionary War, the Marines were a small group of young men chosen simply on the basis of their shooting accuracy. The Marine unit John Gettys was listed with, Captain Mullan's Company of Marines, was a group of sharpshooters who accompanied ships during the war.

In addition to the list of York County Battalions, John appeared on a muster roll taken at Tun Tavern in Philadelphia in December of that year. Tun Tavern was well known as the tavern where the Marines met. That was, however, the last time John Gettys was listed in the Revolutionary War records, at all. Colonial tax records taken from 1779-1783 did not

---

[68] United States. The National Archives. "Revolutionary War pension and Bounty Land Warrant Application Files." Publication M804. Catalog ID 300022. *Case files of Pension and Bounty-Land Warrant Applications Based on Revolutionary Service, Compiled ca. 1800-ca.1912 Documenting the Period ca. 1775-ca. 1900.* Washington: NARA, n.d. Print. ." *Footnote.com.* Web 8 May 2011.

[69] Montgomery, Thomas Lynch, Ed. Pennsylvania Historical and Museum Commission. "Battalions Not Stated York County Militia." *Pennsylvania Archives.* Series 6, Vol. II. Harrisburg: Harrisburg P. Co., State Printer, 1906. 807-872.

[70] Egle, William Henry, Ed. Pennsylvania Historical and Museum Commission. "Miscellaneous Rolls of Associators, Militia and Flying Camp, 1776-1783." *Pennsylvania Archives.* Series 2, Vol. XV. Harrisburg: Harrisburg P. Co., State Printer, 1893..641, 643.

record any John Gettys in the area.[71] In addition, John Gettys was listed in his older sister Martha Gettys Holland's family Bible as dying on April 12 or 19, 1777.[72] It was possible that John Gettys died in camp or was killed in action. However, as very little was known about John, it was also possible that the John Gettys from York was another young man, and James' brother simply died of illness or other causes.

Perhaps the most surprising evidence of family dedication to the American Revolutionary War came in the unveiling of the crippling wounds James' father, Samuel Gettys, received during his volunteer fighting. Samuel appears on a list of soldiers to receive special compensation for severe injuries as a result of their contribution to the Revolutionary War. This was termed the second Act of Congress on September 29, 1789, authorizing the Federal government to compensate "Invalids who were wounded and disabled during the late war."[73] Unfortunately, Samuel never received his compensation as it was distributed in March, 1791, a year following his death. Thus, pensioner "Geddes, Samuel" appears as "deceased."[74]

---

[71] Egle, William Henry, Ed. Pennsylvania Historical & Museum Commission. "Provincial Papers: Returns of Taxables of the County of York, for the Years 1779, 1780, 1781, 1782 and 1783." *Pennsylvania Archives*. Harrisburg: State of Pennsylvania, 1897. 157,318,391,627,737.

[72] Martha Gettys Holland Family Bible. *Courtesy of* ACHS. Gettys File.

[73] Linn, John B. and William H. Egle, eds. Pennsylvania Historical and Museum Commission. "Muster Rolls of Ranging Companies, & C., with lists of Pennsylvania Pensioners in 1789 and 1813: Pennsylvania Pensioners, 1789." *Pennsylvania Archives*. Series 2, Vol. XI. Harrisburg: Lane S. Hart, State Printer, 1880. 747-751.

[74] Ibid. 751.

CHAPTER FOUR

Founding of Gettysburg
and Adams County

SHORTLY AFTER THE REVOLUTIONARY WAR began, it was evident that the colonies needed some form of unified currency. States' funds were used to outfit and pay soldiers, feed and supply them, and repair and replace properties damaged in battles. Farmers and shopkeepers such as James' father, Samuel, supplied goods far more frequently than they were paid. On July 21, 1775, after months of discussions and complaints, the Continental Congress authorized the printing and signing of paper bills of credit called Continental Currency.[75]

The paper bills of credit were modeled after the Spanish monetary system; however, the Continental Currency was not intended to stay in circulation for long. The premise behind these bills of credit was that the individual states collected them when citizens paid taxes, and in turn, submitted them to the Congress for credit. Congress then kept the Continental Currency, gradually removing all the bills from circulation. The plan failed, miserably. The first Continental Currency bills were issued between June 2, 1779, and November 29, 1779. Soon, there were more than 2 million in circulation with nothing backing them. The Continental Currency bills quickly devalued, at the lowest point falling to 40-1 against silver, hence the saying "not worth a Continental."[76] In the meantime, soldiers and merchants who were paid in this currency were exchanging bills that carried little value. These bills circulated throughout the colonies, and the last men or merchants stuck with them lost tremendous amounts of money.

---

[75] United States. United States Department of Treasury. "History 1600-1799." 13 Nov. 2010 Web. 20 March 2011.
[76] Ibid.

Merchants, shopkeepers, and business men who accepted Continental Currency were hard pressed to make up the losses they incurred. The value decreased, continually, and despite speculation otherwise, it never rebounded. To compound the problem, trade with Britain and most countries was at a stand still. Goods were scarce, and each community depended on its own ability to produce enough food, clothing, and farm supplies, as needed. Coin money was limited to what was already in circulation prior to the start of the war. Naturally, the prices of goods available increased, not only for the consumer, but also for the shopkeeper who supplied them. As the shopkeepers and business men raised their prices, the customers went into debt. Customer accounts went unpaid, and business owners, themselves, went broke. As a tavern owner, shopkeeper, and suppler to the militia and Army, James' father, Samuel, fell victim to the downward economic spiral. By the 1780's, Samuel Gettys was seriously in debt.

Unable to pay his loans and his suppliers, Samuel was sued in the York County Courts. Between 1783 and 1785, at least 10 lawsuits were filed against him. The debt was overwhelming, over 8000 pounds.[77] Sheriff William Bailey seized Samuel's land, divided it into parcels, and advertised its sale. However, Samuel's farm was large, and the land market was depressed, which prolonged the court cases and the settlements. The largest suit filed for 6000 pounds against Samuel continued into April of 1787. The court costs and attorney fees only extended Samuel's debt.

---

[77] York County Archives. "York County Court Common Pleas Docket July Term 1783." *York County Archives*. n.d. Web. 25 March 2011. 4, 21,27.; York County Archives. "York County Court Common Pleas Docket January Term 1784." *York County Archives*. n.d. Web. 25 March 2011. 103,109.; York County Archives. "York County Court Common Pleas Docket April Term 1784." *York County Archives*. n.d. Web. 25 March 2011. 155.; York County Archives. "York County Court Common Pleas Docket July Term 1784." *York County Archives*. n.d. Web. 25 March 2011. 230,259.; York County Archives. "York County Court Common Pleas Docket October Term 1784." *York County Archives*. n.d. Web. 25 March 2011. 303.; York County Archives. "York County Court Common Pleas Docket January Term 1785." *York County Archives*. n.d. Web. 25 March 2011. 345.

As Samuel's land was divided and sold piece by piece, young James Gettys purchased 116 acres of it. The deed was officially executed in the York County Court of Common Pleas on October 9, 1786. The "Tract of land Situated in Cumberland Township in the County aforesaid" was sold to "James Gettys for the Sum of Seven Hundred and ninety Pounds lawful money of Pennsylvania."[78] The land included the popular crossroads of York Road and Black Gap Road [Baltimore Road] which was one of the busiest intersections in the area. This tract was the most valuable, in terms of trade and commerce. It also included Samuel's home and his tavern. The relationship between the legal authorities and the Gettys family was not antagonistic, however; each party maintained mutual respect. With wagon travel and trade well developed, 4 area mills producing wood and woolens, and the busy Gettys Tavern, James Gettys made a decision that set the course for the future.

James devised a plan for taking his 116 acres and laying out a town with an organized community and much needed services for the rising population. One common method of selling property at that time was via lottery where the land owner divided his land into lots, each with specified parameters, and created a map showing each lot available. The land owner then sold tickets to area residents and people interested in owning a piece of the newly developing town. A lottery was held and tickets were drawn for each lot. The winner of the lot was given a certain amount of time to purchase it, at which point he or she owed the price of the lot and the quit rent (for taxes). Sometimes ticket holders were afforded the right to purchase in the future, so long as they paid their quit rent to the land owner on time.

James sold lottery tickets for approximately 220 lots and held his drawing in 1786, the same year the courts issued his official deed. This was recognized as the official founding of the town. James had a tremendous amount of business savvy for his young age. Even after York County recognized his ownership of the land, James requested a deed from the Penns acknowledging the land was in his

---

[78] York County Archives. "York County Court Common Pleas Docket October 1786." *York County Archives*. n.d. Web. 25 March 2011. 191.

possession. On April 17, 1787, in Philadelphia, John Penn and John Penn, Jr., completed and signed the official document recognizing the transferring of ownership to James Gettys. It was entered into the York County Court records on April 18, 1787.[79]

After the lottery was held, the lottery ticket holders were slow converting their tickets into sales. No doubt the expense of building another home from scratch kept many of them from realizing their dreams. Within the first year, only 9 of the 210 ticket holders purchased the lots they won.[80] Not all ticket holders lived in the immediate vicinity, so James put an ad in the Carlisle Gazette in September 24, 1787, which appeared in the October 3rd edition. In the ad, James reminded ticket holders that their deeds were ready, and their purchase money and quit rents were due. He emphasized, ". . . it is expected that every one will be punctual in discharging the same immediately."[81] Clearly, he recognized the slow rate of sales. By 1790, two years later, only 17 of the 210 lots were sold.[82]

Not all of the legal parameters of James Gettys' lottery are clear. However, it had a definitive time table in which the ticket holders were required to respond. One year after the lottery was held, James began deeding lots, directly, to people other than the original ticket holders. Simultaneously, James was saving some of the lots for his children; his brother William's children; his sister Elizabeth's two daughters; and two of the Vance girls, previously his father's wards. In fact, James Gettys was so gracious that he even sold lots to William Bailey, the Sheriff who seized the land from Samuel in the first place. The legal system was simply a system. It, in no way, interfered with the community's respect and support for one another.

---

[79] York County Archives. "Grantee Deed Index 1749-1912: G Given Name A-Z." *York County Archives*. n.d. Web. 28 Jan. 2011.

[80] Long, Williams J. Misc. Notes. Gettysburg Lots. Adams County Historical Society. Gettysburg: ACHS, 1974. Cited hereafter as Long, William J. *Courtesy of ACHS.*

[81] "James Gettys." Advertisement. *Carlisle Gazette.* 3 Oct. 1787. Print. *Courtesy of ACHS.*

[82] Long, William J. *Courtesy of ACHS.*

Likewise, nearby towns such as Littlestown, Hunterstown, Abbottstown, and New Oxford already established themselves. With these and many area townships growing, there was a very practical need for access to county services. Traveling to York to file legal documents or attend a meeting took an entire day. That meant accommodations, meals, and traveling back home. Conducting business transactions, as well as keeping law and order in a town without a courthouse, became difficult and time consuming.

Are citizens appealed to the Governor of Pennsylvania to split York and several other counties into separate entities in order to create an area court house and other public service facilities. On January 22, 1800, Governor McKean approved an Act of the General Assembly allowing another county to be formed from part of York.[83] The county was named Adams after the President at the time, John Adams.[84] In the interest of making Gettysburg the county seat, James and several prominent area men already set aside land and money for creating much needed public service buildings. In January of 1799, James promised to donate to the new county the much needed lots for a "gaol" (jail) and courthouse, as well as the right to collect taxes and quit rents on 200 of the town's lots, contingent on "Gettystown" becoming the Adams County seat.[85] Other prominent area men pledged private donations totaling $7,000 for public buildings. Those men included Henry Hoke, James Scott, William McClellan, George Kerr, William McPherson, Alexander Cobean, Alexander Irwin, Alexander Russell, Walter Smith, William Hamilton, John Myers, Emannuel Zeigler, and Samuel Sloan.[86] The commonwealth was impressed with the commitment of the people of Gettysburg, granted the town the county seat.

---

[83] MacKinney, Gertrude, Ed. *Pennsylvania* Historical & Museum Commission. "Executive Minutes of Governor Thomas McKean 1799-1808." *Pennsylvania Archives*. Series 9, Vol. III. Harrisburg: State of Pennsylvania, 1931. 1587.

[84] Pennsylvania Historical & Museum Commission. "Adams County." *Pennsylvania State Archives*. n.c. Web. 19 April 2011.

[85] Adams County Historical Society,. Comp. *Adams County Deed Book A*.66-68. 24 Jan. 1799. Print.

[86] *History of Cumberland and Adams Counties, Pennsylvania*, .41.

CHAPTER FIVE

James Gettys the Civil Servant

ON JANUARY 24, 1800, TWO days after the official formation of the new Adams County, Governor McKean appointed a fellow Democratic-Republican, James Duncan, for Prothonotary. Duncan was also appointed to cover various clerk positions including Clerk of Court, General Quarter Sessions of Peace and Jail Delivery; Clerk of Orphans Court; Clerk of Courts of Oyer and Terminer holden by Judges of Court of Common Pleas; Register of Wills; Grantor of Letters of Administration; and Recorder of Deeds.[87] Suffice to say that all paperwork for the Adams County Courts crossed the desk of James Duncan. This maneuver ensured McKean more control over the heavily populated Federalist county.

The Governor also accepted and appointed a mix of other trustworthy and established men from the area to fill high positions. In April, William Scott, William Gilleland, and John Agnew were appointed Associate Judges of Court of Common Pleas. In December, 10 men were appointed Justices of the Peace for various townships within Adams County.[88] The expediency of the appointments was the result of years of community organization and resolve, and the work of men wholly dedicated to establishing a well rounded county for all of its people.

One major difficulty was evident, however. Adams County did not have a courthouse to try cases and house the newly appointed officials. As one of the provisions in James Gettys' deed to the county trustees was for one lot for the "gaol" or jail, the land was procured, and the

---

[87] MacKinney, Gertrude, Ed. Pennsylvania Historical & Museum Commission. "Executive Minutes of Governor Thomas McKean 1799-1808." *Pennsylvania Archives*. Series 9, Vol. III. Harrisburg: State of Pennsylvania, 1931. 1588.
[88] Ibid. 1623-1696.

first court house and jail were in the official planning processes.[89] Conversely, building a new courthouse/ jail was time consuming and required support and cooperation from the entire county, not just a select few people. County residents pulled together and coordinated resources, starting with the donated lot, extending to pledges for money, and ending with contributions of supplies and labor. The first Adams County courthouse was completed in 1804. It was a two story brick building located in the center of the town square, with the front doors facing Baltimore Street.[90] During the building process, court sessions were held in private homes. The prisoners were housed in jail cells added to the Alms-house.[91] From beginning to end, the county building, indeed the whole process, was successful as a result of the cooperation and collaboration of its proud owners, the citizens of the newly formed Adams County.

During the construction of the county's court house and gaol, elections for various civil service positions were held. Much like elections today, candidates for various town positions advertised their run for candidacy. However, unlike today, the context of the advertisements was subdued and humble. The candidate often stated he was offering his name for the upcoming elections, in response to requests made for him to do so. In addition, the focus of an ad was personal, with the candidate offering pledges of dedication, loyalty, and trust.

In the 1803 nominations for county positions, James Gettys was asked to run for Sheriff. He humbly accepted. In an advertisement dated February 25, 1803, James officially offered himself for candidacy. In the wording of the ad, James appeared both surprised and honored by the request. He commented that he was fortunate enough to obtain the position of candidacy and vowed to be "duty bound to discharge

---

[89] Adams County Historical Society,. Comp. *Adams County Deed Book A.66-68.* 24 Jan. 1799. Print.

[90] "Adams County: County Govt Begins. Court-house, Jail and Alms-house Built." *Gettysburg Compiler, January 23, 1900.* Print. *Gettysburgtimes.com.* Web 27 April 2011. 5,8.

[91] Ibid.

it with candor and fidelity."[92] James' ad ended with the closing, "I am, Gentlemen with the groatest [greatest] sincerity, Your Obedient, Humble Servant."[93]

Following the primary election, Colonel James Gettys and James Horner were the two final candidates for the position of Sheriff, each obtaining enough votes for a run in the general election. It was clear that the reporter for the local newspaper, *The Gazette*, was not pleased that two prominent men were in the running, however, as he complained bitterly and theorized on honor versus profit. The reporter then ended his column by ranting, "O how it GALLS me!!!"[94] It was unclear whether the Gazette reporter ruminated or merely reacted without thinking. In the end, however, the people of Adams County disagreed with The Gazette reporter. They voted for James Gettys, and hence, he became Sheriff for a period of 3 years.

On Tuesday, October 18, 1803, Governor McKean officially announced the appointments of James Gettys, Sheriff, and John Arndt, Coroner, for Adams County. The Governor officially accepted the "Bond and recognizance" put forth by James and approved him for the position.[95] The bond referenced by the Governor was an $8000 surety required by the Commonwealth prior to acceptance of the position. James secured the bond on October 15, 1803, through bondsmen Walter Smith and Jacob Sell.[96] As the bond surely cost James a minimum of fees and interest, the requirement negated The Gazette reporter's earlier accusation of James seeking the position for profit.

---

[92] Gettys, James qtd. in Advertisement. *Gettysburg Gazette*, 27 May 1803. 4. Print. *Gettysburgtimes.com*. Web 18 April 2011.

[93] Ibid

[94] "Editorial Response." *Gettysburg Gazette*, June 17, 1803. 3. Print. *Gettysburgtimes.com*. Web. 19 April 2011.

[95] MacKinney, Gertrude, Ed. Pennsylvania Historical & Museum Commission. "Executive Minutes of Governor Thomas McKean 1799-1808." *Pennsylvania Archives*. Series 9, Vol. III. Harrisburg: State of Pennsylvania, 1931. 1969-1970.

[96] Adams County Historical Society. Comp. *Adams County Deed Book B*. Gettysburg: ACHS, 1803+. 15 October 1803. 198.

In 1806, Pennsylvania's House of Representatives officially incorporated the town of Gettysburg, making it a borough. The act also regulated the procedure for voting in officials, as well as establishing the titles of the official positions, themselves. Being elected to a borough position by the townspeople was considered an honor, yet also a duty. In fact, as per the act, if a citizen of Gettysburg was elected, he must serve in the official position or face penalties.[97]

The first meeting of the Town Council of the Borough of Gettysburg was held on May 21, 1806, at the home of William McClellan. The group was highly organized and appointed positions, immediately. James Gettys was unanimously appointed both Town Clerk and Treasurer. He was required to post another bond, this one for $1000. In return for his duties, James was compensated "two and one half per centum on all monies he shall receive on account of the Borough of Gettysburg."[98] Sureties were common in positions involving the exchange of money. The payment for duties was, most likely, an incentive for the Treasurer to collect cash money rather than start accounts.

During the first year as a borough, the Town Council set the pace by ordering a "valuation of property" for road taxes; purchasing a fire engine and apparatus; creating a dog registration; and preventing swine from "running at large within the borough."[99] In addition, the Town Council was ahead of many towns in banning the disposal of trash, animal carcasses, and "excrement" into the streets.[100] Such ordinances went a long way in the prevention of disasters and illnesses in town.

In 1807, James Gettys was elected to a borough position, again. This time, he was elected to the Town Council.[101] The activities of the council decreased, with primary duties centering on the valuation and

---

[97] Commonwealth of Pennsylvania. "March 10, 1806." The statutes at large of Pennsylvania from 1682-1809. Harrisburg: State of Pennsylvania, 1915. Print. Documents #124, 129. University of Pittsburgh Library. Archive.org. Web. 17 May 2011.

[98] Borough of Gettysburg. *Gettysburg Minute Book 1806-1840.* 1.

[99] Ibid. 2-3.

[100] Ibid. 8.

[101] Ibid. 13.

taxation of properties. The monies were used for the upkeep of roads and, at times, referenced in the minute book as the road tax.

James held positions in the borough two more times. In 1812, he was one of several fire company directors. He and Alexander Cobean, two of the most influential men in the town, were responsible for the Bucket Company answering all fire calls east of the court house. The borough's Town Council was so committed to protecting the townspeople that all councilmen were responsible for ensuring the town's safety. In 1815, James became the Burgess for the borough, a position he held until the day he died. Two days following his death, the Town Council appointed "James Dobbin Esq. Burgess of the Borough of Gettysburg in the place of James Gettys Deces'd."[102] The duties of the Burgess necessitated a quick transition. The minutes thereafter clearly reflected a change recording style and substance.

While it is difficult to imagine such an intense level of public service and commitment, especially in a time in history when public service meant personal inconvenience, James Gettys' achievements were not limited to local service. From 1807-1809, James was elected to the House of Representatives of Pennsylvania. The General Assembly met in Lancaster. During that time period, trade in the Commonwealth continued growing. Thus, the legislature established Pennsylvania creeks and rivers as "public roads" freeing up the waterways for the shipping of goods and materials.[103] Notably, the most significant piece of legislation passed during James' tenure was the 1807 statute allowing "aliens in certain cases to purchase and hold real estate within this commonwealth."[104] In the 1807 statute, Pennsylvania joined other states in slowly easing the harshness of the Federal Alien and Sedition Acts of 1798.

---

[102] Ibid. 71.

[103] *Laws of the Commonwealth of Pennsylvania, From the Fourteenth Day of October, One Thousand Seven Hundred.* Philadelphia: Bioren, 1810. Google Book Search. Web 8 May 2011. 359+.

[104] Commonwealth of Pennsylvania. "February 10, 1807." The statutes at large of Pennsylvania from 1682-1809. Harrisburg: State of Pennsylvania, 1915. Document #343. Print. University of Pittsburgh Library. Archive.org.

There was no doubt as to James Gettys' political astuteness. While there were men in the county who held more money in their coffers, few held more social and political power. James' public persona engendered trust and admiration, yet he remained humble and gracious. He never felt he was above others, and to this he never ceased educating himself. His library contained books on Pennsylvania law, as well as essays and sermons on public behavior. Two such books in James Gettys' library were Knox's essays and *Smith's Sermons.*[105] Knox's essays were large in number and most likely serialized, covering subjects paramount to the social behavior of a public figure. For example, No. 122 "On the Importance of Governing the Temper," guided men away from maintaining an "ill temper," and suggested adopting a "culture of understanding."[106] Similarly, No. 124, "On the Influence of Politics as a Subject of Conversation, on the State of Literature," emphasized the belief during the time that "Interest in politics is healthy in that it reflects ardent love of freedom, a Gift from God."[107] Lastly but quite interestingly, James read *Smith's Sermons,* a well know series written by William Smith, the founder of Washington College, who was born in Aberdeen, Scotland. At the culmination of the Revolutionary War, debate ensued as to Smith's allegiance to the independence movement. At any rate, Smith was favored by George Washington, hence, favored by many of Washington's admirers such as James.

---

[105] McClean, Wm. Archibald, Ed. "General James Gettys, Proprietor." *Compiler Scrapbook.* Gettysburg: Compiler, 1908. 12-13. *Courtesy of* ACHS.

[106] Ferguson, James, Esq. The British Essayists with Prefaces, Biographical, Historical, and Critical. 2nd ed., vol. III. London: Richardson and Co., 1823. #122.

[107] Ibid. #124.

CHAPTER SIX

Investments for Community Benefit

IT CAN BE SAID THAT James Gettys knew a good investment when he saw one, but what was extraordinary was his never ending investments in his community. Gettysburg and the surrounding towns were growing in population. As commerce increased between towns, so did the need for reliable roads. Roads consisting of dug out dirt paths were neither wide enough for heavy traffic flow nor reliable enough to depend on for trade.

James Gettys and eight other local men, community leaders in name and position, presented a plan to Governor McKean for building a major road from Gettysburg through Petersburg (now Littlestown) and down to the Maryland state line. The Governor approved of the plan and passed an Act of Assembly on April 7, 1807, creating the Gettysburg and Petersburg Turnpike Company. The commissioners were James Gettys, James McSherry, John Shoop, Jacob Winteroff, Alexander Cobean, and Henry Hoke.[108]

The Gettysburg and Petersburg Turnpike Company was responsible for raising the money for purchasing the stone, tools, and labor for completing the task. James was listed as Treasurer, and he and the commissioners sold shares of the company at $100 each to raise the funds.[109] Building roads in the early 1800s was daunting work, slow and difficult. When the road was completed, it was gated, and access permitted upon collection of a toll. Church goers and funeral processions usually passed without charge. Regardless of the traffic, start-up costs were so high that dividends were not always guaranteed.

---

[108] MacKinney, Gertrude, Ed. Pennsylvania Historical & Museum Commission. "Executive Minutes of Governor Thomas McKean 1808." *Pennsylvania Archives.* Series 9, Vol. IV. Harrisburg: State of Pennsylvania, 1931. 2521.

[109] "Turnpikes." *Gettysburg Gazette, February 10, 1881.* Print. *Gettysburgtimes. com.* Web 19 April 2011. 1.

The Gettysburg and Petersburg Turnpike proved not only a benefit to the community, but also an investment well made. The much needed road was heavily traveled. By May of 1812, the Gettysburg and Petersburg Turnpike Company issued dividends of 1 and ¼ per cent of the capital stock.[110]

Simultaneously, James assisted in forming another turnpike company called the Gettysburg and Blacks' Tavern Turnpike Company. The proposal detailed a road stretching from Gettysburg to Black's Tavern. The plan was accepted by Governor Simon Snyder. The Act of Assembly was passed on February 6, 1811, and the formation of the Gettysburg and Blacks' Tavern Turnpike Company was official.[111] Shares were issued following additional supplemental provisions in March. On April 18, 1811, the shareholders were officially documented by the Governor. James Gettys and James Black each bought 4 shares, the largest per person listed. There were 19 shareholders in total.[112] Gettys was not, however, an officer of this company. He did not handle the treasury or issue the contracts.

As the communities took advantage of their growth in trade and stature, the increase in commerce meant an increase in income. This, in turn, meant a need for an expansion of services and a means of securing what lead the demand: money. Shop owners took huge risks closing up shop and taking all the sales for the day home with them for safe keeping. The only other alternative at the time was traveling to another city and depositing the money in a bank. If the depositor arrived safely with his money still on his person, he then deposited it without any reward or interest, only to return shortly thereafter to withdraw it to pay his bills. Without a doubt, Adams County was in need of a bank of its own. Not only would a local bank decrease the risks for shop owners and self employed laborers, but simultaneously, it would provide a legitimate manner by which people borrow and pay

---

[110] Ibid.

[111] MacKinney, Gertrude, Ed. Pennsylvania Historical & Museum Commission. "Executive Minutes of Governor Simon Snyder 1812-1814." *Pennsylvania Archives.* Series 9, Vol. IV. Harrisburg: State of Pennsylvania, 1931. 2973-4.

[112] Ibid.

back loans. Thus, in 1809, the concept of founding a Gettysburg bank began took shape.

The founders of this new county bank were the men most trusted in the county. The men were financially secured, themselves, each with enough money for the initial investment. On April 26, 1809, James Gettys sold one lot on the town square to the newly forming bank organizers.[113] The process was, once again, slow. The state legislators passed an Act of General Assembly allowing the formation of a bank in March of 1813; however, it was vetoed by Governor Snyder.[114] One year later, Governor Snyder's veto was overridden. In the official minutes of Friday, April 29, 1814, Governor Snyder acknowledged the Act of General Assembly passed, and decreed that a bank be established in the District of Adams County.[115] Even though the bank was proposed and supported by men from various towns and locals in the county, the lot was donated by James Gettys and in Gettysburg; therefore, the bank was named the Bank of Gettysburg.

On March 21, 1814, the founding members issued subscriptions for stock at the price of $50.00 per share. The stock was sold at several locations, one in each of the relative communities.[116] James Gettys purchased 50 shares; however, he was not among the top shareholders. Several men purchased 100 shares, indicating that while James was one of the most respected and trusted men in the area, he was not the wealthiest. On May 26th, an election for Bank Directors was held at the Adams County Court House. The voters chose James Gettys, Alexander Cobean, Robert Hayes, Barnhart Gilbert, Ralph Lashells, Walter Smith, Jacob Eyster, Andrew Will, Amos McGinley, Michael Slagle, John Dickson, William Wierman, and Patrick Reed. Alexander

---

[113] McSherry, William, L.L.D. *History of the Bank of Gettysburg 1814-1864: The Gettysburg National Bank 1864-1914 of Gettysburg, Pennsylvania.* Gettysburg: The Gettysburg National Bank, 1914. Google Book Search. Web. 8 May 2011. 100. Cited hereafter as McSherry.

[114] Ibid. 11.

[115] MacKinney, Gertrude, Ed. Pennsylvania Historical & Museum Commission. "Executive Minutes of Governor Simon Snyder 1812-1814." *Pennsylvania Archives.* Series 9, Vol. V. Harrisburg: State of PA, 1931. 3511-12.

[116] McSherry. 12.

Cobean was elected President, and John B. McPherson was elected Cashier.[117]

Interestingly enough, James also purchased 4 shares in the newly formed bank under the auspicious of guardian for Jane and Sarah Sloan.[118] Without hesitation, James was not only supplying the basic necessities for his wards to survive, but helping the children establish a future as part of the community.

---

[117] Ibid.. 21-22.
[118] Ibid. 12.

CHAPTER SEVEN

General James Gettys Dies;
the Legend Lives On

WHILE THE COLONIAL DAYS SET the pace for political and civil advancement in America, that was not the case on the medical front. There were no antibiotics of any kind. Penicillin wasn't formulated, yet, neither was aspirin, and basic vaccinations were new and not prevalent in America. Death was an every day occurrence, even in a small town. Many children did not live to adulthood, and adults often died simply from living with or near another ill person. In fact, early American houses often had one door that was wider than the others called the coffin door. Gettysburg was not spared this exposure. As a thoroughfare for many travelers, if a particularly viral germ or bug found its way into the town, it was virtually impossible to avoid exposure. Thus was the case in 1815.

In the spring of 1815, Typhus cholera outbreaks occurred in several states, including Pennsylvania and Maryland. In fact, Typhus was recorded at epidemic levels in two counties on the Maryland coast.[119] Baltimore was a major shipping port, and Pennsylvanians made frequent trips there for purchasing supplies. Likewise, the Pennsylvania militia units just returned from defending the port from the British at the culmination of the War of 1812. The people of these two states were continually in contact with one another; therefore, they unfortunately shared mutual contagions.

In an article written in 1898 by the Surgeon General of the United States Army, George Steinberg, M.D., LLC, Dr. Steinberg examined the medical history of the 19th century. One main phenomenon Steinberg observed was that Typhus Fever was the most prevalent and most

---

[119] Cordell, Eugene Fauntleroy, M.D. *The medical annals of Maryland, 1799-1899.* Baltimore, 1903. Google Book Search. Web. 21 May 2011. 680-1.

fatal in colder climates and environments where people were in close quarters, and ventilation was poor.[120] Those were the conditions in the spring of 1815 when General James Gettys and many in the Gettys household died.

In addition to the documented prevalence of Typhus during the time period, descriptions of the illness or "fever" that lingered in the Gettys household was typical of the disease. The Gettys family was continually surrounded by people, both locals and travelers. The disease spread quickly. Likewise, the family had a fair amount of animals on the property: dogs, horses, cattle, pigs, and fowl. Fleas and lice carried the disease, and often multiplied on animals in the barns, especially the fowl. Once spread to a human, Typhus, remained in the environment - in the dust and the air - quickly spreading from person to person.

As was typical with Typhus Fever, adults were especially stricken. James' sister Martha Gettys Holland died first on March 10th, 1815.[121] Her death was followed by their mother, Isabella, on March 12th. General James died on March 13th.[122] His wife, Mary Todd Gettys, died on March 17th. Nine other people in the area died that week, including Baltzer Spangler McClellan, the 21 year old son of William McClellan.[123] Within two weeks, Isabella's caretaker and granddaughter, Sally Fleming, was stricken and died (April 6th, 1815). Then Polly and Margaret Horner, the wife and daughter of James' close friend Robert Horner (who coincidentally purchased James' horse at the auction held on the Gettys' property following James' death), died on April 9th and April 1st, respectively.[124] When the crisis subsided, James' two sons, Robert Todd and James, Jr., had survived, and their

---

[120] Sternberg, M.D., LLD., George M. Surgeon General US Army. "The Etiology and Geographic Distribution of Infectious Diseases. *Popular Science Monthly.* Jan. 1898. Google Book Search. Web. 21 May 2011. 295.

[121] Martha Gettys Holland Family Bible. *Courtesy of* ACHS.

[122] "Gettysburg." *Adams Centinel.* 15 March 1815.*Courtesy of* ACHS. Gettys File.

[123] "Deaths." *Adams Centinel,* 22 March 1815. Print. *Gettysburgtimes.com.* Web. 21 May 2011.

[124] "Gettysburg." *Adams Centinel.*19 April 1815. *Courtesy of* ACHS. Gettys File; Gravestone of Margaret Horner. Blacks Cemetery. Gettysburg, PA.

financial inheritance was placed in the care of the executor, Alexander Cobean.

In James Gettys' obituary in the *Adams Centinel*, the journalist stated that General James fell ill on Sunday, March 5, in the evening. He attended church that day, and was ill with fever by nightfall.[125] Six days later, obviously realizing he was dying, he sent for his solicitor and wrote his will. General James, usually a prolific writer, wrote one of the shortest pieces of his life. His wife was not ill, as of yet, and he left all his possessions to her and their two living children, two sons, to be shared equally. Mary was also named as an executor, along with General James' close friend, Alexander Cobean.[126] Tragically, Mary Gettys became fatally ill immediately following James' death.

When Mary Gettys passed away, James, Jr., and Robert Todd were yet too young to live on their own. James, Jr., was sixteen, and Robert Todd was six. All property owned by their father went to them. There were also family debts and loans. Like any businessman, General James was in the midst of several business transactions, and the loans had to be repaid. In the years prior to his death, he sold off one of the two houses he owned, his 100 acres of farmland, and eight of the ten remaining Gettysburg plots.[127] Upon his death, his estate consisted of one home, one barn, and 2 remaining town lots.[128] Three years later, in 1818, the executor sold off the remaining town lots, presumably for the support of the two boys. The Gettys' home was transferred to James, Jr.'s name and was listed in the tax assessment under James Gettys (heir).[129] At that point, James, Jr., was 19 years old and still living in Gettysburg.

By 1822, seven years after his father's death, James, Jr., established himself in the community as a tanner, one who works leather. The business was lucrative, and he kept possession of the house and purchased two additional lots for a larger "tanyard" or tannery of his

[125] "Gettysburg." *Adams Centinel*.15 March 1815. *Courtesy of* ACHS. Gettys File.

[126] McClean, William. Archibald, Ed. "James Gettys' Will." *Compiler Scrapbook*. Gettysburg: Compiler, 1908. 18-19. *Courtesy of* ACHS. Gettys File.

[127] Borough of Gettysburg. *Gettysburg Minute Book 1806-1840*. 49+, 58+, 77.

[128] Ibid. 77.

[129] Ibid. 102+.

own.[130] In 1823, the tannery business was successful enough that he also purchased an additional 60 acres of land.[131] He married Hanna Dickson, and began a new life as a husband and a father.

However, regardless of James, Jr.'s, attempt to create stability in Gettysburg, his strides were in vane. On July 8, 1824, his 3 year old daughter Mary Jane Gettys died of an unknown illness. On November 18 of that same year, his 10 month old son, John Gettys, passed away, as well.[132] Compounding his strife, James, Jr.'s, only surviving sibling, Robert Todd, died 3 years later, in 1827.[133] At that point, he sold off the Gettys' home, the land, and most of the tannery.[134] After James, Jr., buried his brother Todd, he sold what remained of the tannery, and he and his wife moved from Gettysburg to Tennessee.[135]

---

[130] Ibid. 120.

[131] Ibid. 121.

[132] "Died-" *Republican Compiler, Wednesday, July 14, 1824.* 3. Print. *Gettysburgtimes. com.* Web. 30 May 2011.; "Died." *Republican Compiler, Wednesday, November 24, 1824.* 3. Print. *Gettysburgtimes.com.* Web. 31 May 2011.

[133] "Died." *Adams Sentinel.* 21 March 1827. Print. *Gettysburgtimes.com.* Web. 31 May 2011.

[134] Borough of Gettysburg. *Gettysburg Minute Book 1806-1840.* 150, 160.

[135] Ibid. 160, 174.

CHAPTER EIGHT

Ties to the Civil War and Town

LIFE TENDS TO COME AROUND full circle, and such was the case for the little town of Gettysburg. The town built by a unique group of dedicated, committed people, secured by men who fought in two wars defending its liberty, refused to succumb during the battle of the nation, the Civil War.

While many men with the last name Gettys enlisted and fought in the Civil War, three men, in particular, were directly connected to General James Gettys. The first and perhaps most significant was Lieutenant James R. Gettys, the Tennessee son of James Gettys, Jr., and the grandson of General James Gettys. Lieutenant Gettys enlisted and was discharged as a Private in the Tennessee Union Army, Company C 7th Regiment Mounted Infantry. During his service, he temporarily served as Lieutenant, as the position became vacant. He did so, admirably. While his original enlistment was in Nashville, Tennessee, he spent most of his tour of duty stationed around Athens, Tennessee.[136] He did not, however, see action in Gettysburg.

In addition, General James' brother William, who fought in the Revolutionary War, had two grandsons who were soldiers in the Civil War. The first grandson was the son of James Gettys, II, and Elizabeth Watson Gettys from North Carolina, and he was named William H. Gettys. He joined the Confederate Army early on in the war. He was assigned to Company K 50th Regiment, North Carolina. He died in camp on October 2, 1862. Notice was sent to his mother, Elizabeth shortly thereafter.[137]

---

[136] United States. The National Archives. "Carded Records Showing Military Service of Soldiers Who Fought in Volunteer Organizations During the American Civil War, compiled 1890-1912, documenting period 1861-1866." RG 94, TN Cat.300398. Washington: GPO, n.d. Footnote.com. Web 23 May 2011.

[137] United States. The National Archives. "Unified Papers and Slips Belonging in Confederate Compiled Service Records." Pub. M347, Cat.2133276. Washington: GPA, 1962. 2010 Footnote.com. Web. 2010. 23 May 2011.

William's son Samuel had a son named Migamin Gettys, a North Carolina farmer who enlisted in the Civil War at 44 years old. Ironically, Mig, as he was called, left North Carolina and enlisted with the Tennessee Union Army in a volunteer unit out of Cleveland, Tennessee. Mig was part of Company C 5th Regiment Mounted Infantry.[138] Mig's unit served towards the end of the war guarding the garrison in Georgia. The unit was involved in a skirmish at McLemores Cove. Mig mustered out on February 28, 1865, shortly after the skirmish.[139] His early dismissal indicated he was probably wounded. Mig Gettys did not see action in Gettysburg, either.

In the months after the Battle of Gettysburg, the small town and its surrounding farms showed the massive destruction wrought by war, as well as the need for proper burial of the thousands of men who died during the battle. By the autumn of 1863, Soldiers National Cemetery was established for such purpose. On November 19, 1863, President Abraham Lincoln spoke at the dedication, giving his famous Gettysburg Address and bringing national recognition to the cemetery.

Right next door to the Soldiers National Cemetery and within sight of Lincoln's Gettysburg Address, sat the Evergreen Cemetery, established in 1854 for the residents of Gettysburg. In 1865 during the second anniversary of the founding of the Soldiers National Cemetery, General James Gettys' son, James Gettys, Jr., returned to Gettysburg for a short time and organized the exhumation and reburial of his parents, his two cousins, and his brother from their original resting places to Evergreen. The family church, Gettysburg Presbyterian, had interned its members in two cemeteries, prior: the old Blacks Cemetery three miles outside of town and a newer cemetery next to the second church location on Washington Street and Railroad. The church soon moved to its third and current location on Baltimore Street and High Street. In 1865, all of the buried church members were

---

[138] The National Archives. "Carded Records Showing Military Service of Soldiers Who Fought in Volunteer Organizations During the American Civil War, compiled 1890-1912, documenting period 1861-1866." RG 94, TN Catalog ID#300398. The National Archives.org. The National Archives. Washington. n.d. Footnote.com. Web 23 May 2011.

[139] Ibid.

exhumed from the Washington Street and Railroad Road cemetery and moved to Evergreen Cemetery.[140] The Railroad Road location was in the midst of construction when most of the Gettys family died, thus they were originally buried in the old Blacks Cemetery. As Robert Todd Gettys died in 1827, he was most likely among those exhumed from the Railroad Road cemetery. James, Jr., chose not to exhume his grandmother, Isabella Gettys, allowing her to remain in Blacks Cemetery with her husband, Samuel, who died in 1790. Where the children of James, Jr., were laid to rest remains a mystery today.

Once James, Jr., moved his father, mother, brother, and cousins to Evergreen, he purchased a large memorial for his father and mother. Originally, the monument was 17 feet in height, with a beautiful marble urn on the top and a carved relief depicting the likeness of his father on the side. In subsequent years, the top of the monument fell victim to a storm, leaving what resembled a large obelisk, with the relief still intact.

Behind General James' monument, and to the left, lies a flat stone in memory of James, Jr.'s two cousins, Sally Fleming and Isabella Ewing. While weathered, it can still be read that the stone is "In memory of" Sally Fleming and Isabella Ewing (Sally's sister). Behind General James' monument, and to the right, is an upright marble tombstone dedicated to James Junior's seventeen-year old brother, Robert Todd. The last lines of his stone are eroded from the elements, but careful reading reveals the following:

> *Remember me, as you pass by*
> *As you are now, so once was I*
> *As I am now, so shalt thou be*
> *Prepare for death, & follow me*
> *I've run my race, my pilgrimage*
> *How short my life! How swift my days*
> *My years are few and ended soon*
> *My mourning sun is set to noon*

---

[140] Gettysburg Presbyterian Church. "Tour of Black's Graveyard." *Gettysburg Presbyterian Church Grapevine [Newsletter]*. Gettysburg: GPC. 20 May 2009. 5. Print. Web. 12 June 2011.

The epitaph was humbling and unexpected, as the Gettys family usually had a great sense of humor. When General James' monument was originally placed in Evergreen, it was flanked by a statue of his dog that was said to have worn an identical collar that read, "I'm James Gettys' dog, whose dog are you?"[141] As General James was never a man to wallow in sorrow or self pity, the legend was probably true.

The only known remaining artifact from the Gettys estate is a chair held in the collections of the Adams County Historical Society. The chair, a Windsor style fan-backed chair, has bamboo turned legs, a particularly popular style during the post Revolutionary War period. Chairs were usually made by local furniture makers. One such local furniture maker during James Gettys' time was Gettysburg, resident Edward Davis. In July of 1804, Davis placed an ad in the *Centinel* where he advertised the sale of his locally made Windsor and split-bottom chairs.[142] As James Gettys was known for having his furniture made locally, perhaps Davis or one of his contemporaries made the chair housed at the Adams County Historical Society, today.

Aptly, the small but notable town of Gettysburg, Pennsylvania, continues to thrive. With courage and quiet respect, they honor their forefathers as well as the fallen. It was true that General James Gettys' property was the foundation of the town and that he placed tremendous time, effort, and resources into creating and organizing the newly-formed community. Yet, let it be said that Gettysburg did not rise because of the efforts of one man, alone. The proud, historical town of Gettysburg grew as a result of many of years of work and dedication by a tightly knit community of people who stood by each other while they built their dream.

---

[141] McClean, William. Archibald, Ed. "James Gettys' Will." *Compiler Scrapbook.* Gettysburg: Compiler, 1908. 10-11. *Courtesy of* ACHS. Gettys File.

[142] Davis, Edward. Advertisement. *Centinel.* 20 June 1804. Print. Courtesy of the Adams County Historical Society. Gettysburg File.

A modern photo of General James Gettys' and Mary Gettys' grave memorial. *Photo by Amanda Howlett*

A modern close-up photo of James Gettys' motif on the James
Gettys and Mary Gettys grave memorial. *Photo by Amanda Howlett.*

A modern photo of the gravestone of James' son Robert Todd Gettys, located behind his memorial. *Photo by Amanda Howlett.*

A modern photo of the memorial stone to
James Gettys' nieces Sally Fleming and
Isabella Ewing, located behind his memorial.
Photo by Amanda Howlett.

Memorial marker for James Gettys' parents, Samuel and Isabella Gettys, in Black's Graveyard. Marker dedicated by William Gettys' family. *Photo by Amanda Howlett.*

A modern photo of the memorial plaque
marking the original site of Gettys
family homestead, located in Racehorse
Alley. *Photo by Amanda Howlett.*

GOVERNMENT DOCUMENTS

Adams County Historical Society. Comp. *Adams County Deed Book A.* Gettysburg: ACHS, 1800 +. 24 Jan. 1799.

Adams County Historical Society. Comp. *Adams County Deed Book B.* Gettysburg: ACHS, 1803+. 15 October 1803.

Adams County Historical Society. Comp. "Samuel Gettys Deed." *York County Deed Book D4, 145."* Gettysburg: ACHS. n.d. *Courtesy of* ACHS.

Adams County Historical Society, Comp. "Taxes Cumberland Township 1798." York County Direct Tax 1798. Gettysburg: ACHS, n.d.

Borough of Gettysburg. *Gettysburg Minute Book 1806-1840.* Gettysburg: BOG, 1806-40.

Egle, William Henry. Pennsylvania Historical and Museum Commission. "Caveat Books 1748-1784." *Pennsylvania Archives.* Series 3, Vol. II, Harrisburg: Clarence M. Busch, State Printer, 1894. 329-30.

Egle, William Henry, Ed. Pennsylvania Historical and Museum Commission. "Miscellaneous Rolls of Associators, Militia and Flying Camp, 1776-1783." *Pennsylvania Archives.* Series 2, Vol. XV. Harrisburg: Harrisburg P. Co., State Printer, 1893.

Egle, William Henry, Ed. Pennsylvania Historical & Museum Commission. "Provincial Papers: Returns of Taxables of the County of York, for the Years 1779, 1780, 1781, 1782 and 1783." *Pennsylvania Archives.* Harrisburg: State of Pennsylvania, 1898.

Hoban, Charles F., Ed. Pennsylvania Historical and Museum Commission. "Votes of Assembly 1775." Pennsylvania Archives. Series

8, Vol. VIII. January 7, 1771-September 26, 1776. Harrisburg: State of Pennsylvania, 1935.

Linn, John Blair and William H. Egle, eds. Pennsylvania Historical and Museum Commission. "Colonel William Thompson's Battalion of Riflemen. June 25, 1775-July 1, 1776."*Pennsylvania Archives.* Series 2, Vol. X. Harrisburg: Edwin K. Meyers, State Printer, 1891.

MacKinney, Gertrude, Ed. Pennsylvania Historical & Museum Commission. "Executive Minutes Governor Simon Snyder 1808-1812." Series 9, Vol. IV. Harrisburg: State of Pennsylvania, 1931.

MacKinney, Gertrude, Ed. Pennsylvania Historical & Museum Commission. "Executive Minutes of Governor Simon Snyder 1812-1814." *Pennsylvania Archives.* Series 9, Vol. V. Harrisburg: State of Pennsylvania, 1931.

MacKinney, Gertrude, Ed. Pennsylvania Historical & Museum Commission. "Executive Minutes of Governor Thomas McKean 1799-1808." *Pennsylvania Archives.* Series 9, Vol. III. Harrisburg: State of Pennsylvania, 1931.

MacKinney, Gertrude, Ed. Pennsylvania Historical and Museum Commission. "Executive Minutes of Governor Thomas Mifflin 1790-1792." *Pennsylvania Archives.* Series 9, Vol. I, Harrisburg: State of PA, 1931.

Montgomery, Thomas Lynch, Ed. Pennsylvania Historical and Museum Commission. "Battalions Not Stated York County Militia." *Pennsylvania Archives.* Series 6, Vol. II. Harrisburg: Harrisburg P. Co., State Printer, 1906.

Montgomery, Thomas Lynch, Ed. Pennsylvania Historical and Museum Commission. "Continental Line, 10th Pennsylvania October 25, 1776-January 17, 1781." *Pennsylvania Archives.* Series 5, Vol. III. Harrisburg: Harrisburg P. Co., State Printer, 1906.

Montgomery, Thomas Lynch, ed. Pennsylvania Historical & Museum Commission. "Militia Rolls." *Pennsylvania Archives.* Series 6, Vol. III. Harrisburg: State Printer, 1907.

Montgomery, Thomas Lynch, Ed. Pennsylvania Historical & Museum Commission. "War 1812=1814." *Pennsylvania Archives.* Series 6, Vol. VII. Harrisburg: Harrisburg P. Co., State Printer, 1907.

Montgomery, Thomas Lynch, Ed. Pennsylvania Historical & Museum Commission. "York County Militia 1790-1800." *Pennsylvania Archives.* Series 6, Vol. V. Harrisburg: State of PA, 1907.

Pennsylvania, Board of County Commissioners. "Cumberland Township 1799." *York County Tax Records 1799.*York County Archives. n.d. Microfilm. 6 June 2011. Roll #5227.

Pennsylvania Department of State. "Republica vs. Capt. Alexander Cobean." *Pennsylvania Archives.* Record Group: Dept. of State. Subgroup: Secty of Commonwealth. Series: Court Martial Proceedings. RG 26.4-0460. Box #1. 1790-March 1814.

Pennsylvania Department of State. "Republica vs. Col. James Gettys." *Pennsylvania Archives.* RG: Dept. of State. Subgroup: Secty of Commonwealth. Series: Court Martial Proceedings. RG 26.4-0460. Box #1. 1790-March 1814.

Pennsylvania Historical & Museum Commission. "Adams County." *Pennsylvania Historical & Museum Commission* n.d. Web. 19 April 2011.

Pennsylvania Historical & Museum Commission. "Muster Rolls - Pennsylvania Militia War 1812-1814: With Contemporary Papers and Documents." *Pennsylvania Archives.* series 2, vol. XII. Harrisburg: E.K. Myers, State Printer, 1890.

Pennsylvania Historical & Museum Commission. "Revolutionary War Military Abstract Card File: Items Between Gabell, Thomas and Gaddis, Joseph." *Military Accounts: Militia. Pennsylvania Archives.* n.d.

Web. Feb. 2011. ARIAS: Pennsylvania Digital State Archives. "Military Accounts: Militia."

Pennsylvania Historical and Museum Commission. "Revolutionary War Military Abstract Card File: Items Between Gerum, Thos., and Geyer,Casper. Item 56." *Pennsylvania Digital State Archives*. n.d. Web. Feb. 2011.

United States. The National Archives. "Carded Records Showing Military Service of Soldiers Who Fought in Volunteer Organizations During the American Civil War, compiled 1890-1912, documenting period 1861-1866." RG 94, TN Cat.300398. Washington: GPO, n.d. Footnote.com. Web 23 May 2011.

United States. The National Archives. "Revolutionary War pension and Bounty Land Warrant Application Files." Publication M804. Cat.300022. *Case files of Pension and Bounty-Land Warrant Applications Based on Revolutionary Service, Compiled ca. 1800-ca.1912 Documenting the Period ca. 1775-ca. 1900*. Washington: NARA, n.d. Footnote.com. Web. 8 May 2011.

United States. The National Archives. "Unified Papers and Slips Belonging in Confederate Compiled Service Records." Pub. M347, Cat.2133276. Washington: GPA, 1962. 2010 Footnote.com. Web. 2010. 23 May 2011.

United States. United States Department of Treasury. "History 1600-1799." 13 Nov. 2010 Web. 20 March 2011.

York County Archives. "Grantee Deed Index 1749-1912: G Given Name A-Z." *York County Archives*. n.d. Web. 28 Jan. 2011.

York County Archives. "December 8 1773." *Clerk of Courts Quarter Session Dockets 1749-1876. York County, Pennsylvania. York County Archives*. n.d. Web. 29 Jan. 2011.

York County Archives. "July 29, 1763." *Clerk of Courts Quarter Session Dockets 1749-1876*. York County, Pennsylvania. *York County Archives.* n.d. Web. 29 Jan. 2011.

York County Archives. "June Sessions 1799." *Clerk of Courts Quarter Session Dockets 1749-1876*. York County, Pennsylvania. *York County Archives.* n.d. Web. 29 Jan. 2011.

York County Archives. "March 25 1772." *Clerk of Courts Quarter Session Dockets 1749-1876*. York County, Pennsylvania. *York County Archives.* n.d. Web. 29 Jan. 2011.

York County Archives. "September Sessions 1798." *Clerk of Courts Quarter Session Dockets 1749-1876*. York County, Pennsylvania. *York County Archives.* n.d. Web. 29 Jan. 2011.

York County Archives. "October 1761." *Clerk of Courts Quarter Session Dockets 1749-1876*. York County, Pennsylvania. *York County Archives.* n.d. Web. 29 Jan. 2011.

York County Archives. "July 1783." *York County Court Common Pleas Docket July 1783-July 1785*. York County Archives. n.d. Web. 25 March 2011.

--"January 1784."
--"April 1784."
--"July 1784."
--"October 1784."
--"January 1785."

York County Archives. "York County Court Common Pleas Docket October 1786." *York County Archives.* n.d. Web. 25 March 2011.

York County, PA Board of County Commissioners. "Cumberland Township." *Tax Records Franklin, Monaghan, Warrington, Dover, Newberry, Manchester, Mount Joy, Huntingdon, Straban, Cumberland, Hamilton Bann, and Reading Twps., 1786.* (1). Microfilm. Roll 5222.

Books - Secondary Sources

Bloom, Robert L. A History of Adams County, Pennsylvania 1700-1990. Gettysburg: ACHS, 1992.

Commonwealth of Pennsylvania. "February 10, 1807 #343." The statutes at large of Pennsylvania from 1682-1809. Harrisburg: State of Pennsylvania, 1915. Print. University of Pittsburgh Library. Archive.org.

Commonwealth of Pennsylvania. "March 10, 1806 #124, 129." The statutes at large of Pennsylvania from 1682-1809. Harrisburg: State of Pennsylvania, 1915. Print. University of Pittsburgh Library. Archive. org. Web. 17 May 2011.

Cordell, Eugene Fauntleroy, M.D. *The medical annals of Maryland, 1799-1899*. Baltimore, 1903. Google Book Search. Web. 21 May 2011.

Earle, Alice Morse. Stage Coach and Tavern Days. New York: Macmillan, 1915.

Ferguson, James, Esq. The British Essayists with Prefaces, Biographical, Historical, and Critical. 2nd ed., Vol. III. London: Richardson and Co., 1823.

Gettys, Melissa and Amanda Howlett. "The Military Career of James Gettys." *Adams County History*. Adams County Historical Society, 2017.

Glatfelter, Charles H. and Arthur Weaner. *The Settlers of the Manor of Maske Being the Documentary and Commentary for the Map: The Subdivision of the Manor of Maske*. Gettysburg: ACHS, 1989. *Courtesy of* ACHS.

Glatfelter, Charles H. and Larry Bolin. Adams County Historical Society. *Manor of the Maske: 11-21*. Gettysburg: ACHS, n.d., Cumberland Township Section, 2. *Courtesy of* ACHS.

History of Cumberland and Adams Counties, Pennsylvania. Chicago: Warner Beers, 1886.

Laws of the Commonwealth of Pennsylvania, From the Fourteenth Day of October, One Thousand Seven Hundred. Philadelphia: Bioren, 1810. Google Book Search. Web 8 May 2011.

McSherry, William, L.L.D. History of the Bank of Gettysburg 1814-1864: The Gettysburg National Bank 1864-1914 of Gettysburg, Pennsylvania. Gettysburg: The Gettysburg National Bank, 1914. Google Book Search. Web. 8 May 2011.

Proud, Robert. *History of Pennsylvania 1681-1770*. Vol. I., 1797. Philadelphia: Poulson; Harrisburg: PA State Library, 1967. 246-50.

Sternberg, M.D., LLD., George M. Surgeon General US Army. "The Etiology and Geographic Distribution of Infectious Diseases. Popular Science Monthly. Jan. 1898. Google Book Search. Web. 21 May 2011.

Young, Henry James et al. York County, Pennsylvania, in the American Revolution. Red Series. Vol. III. Gettysburg: ACHS, 1958.

Young, Henry James. York County, Pennsylvania, in the American Revolution: A Source Book. Gettysburg: ACHS, 1935. .

Collections, Documents - Primary Sources

Glatfelter, Dr. Charles. H. Personal Interview. 22 January 2011.

Martha Gettys Holland Family Bible. Courtesy of Adams County Historical Society. Gettys Family File.

W. Arthur Gettys. Letter to author's grandfather, Harold Binkley Gettys. 23 May 1964.

Will of William Gettys. *Rutherford Count North Carolina Record of Wills 1782-1923.* Reel C.086.80001. Courtesy of The Genealogical Society of Old Tryon County, North Carolina, Inc. Forest City, NC.

"Will of Adam Vance." *York County Archives.* June 2011 Pdf. June 2011.

Collections, Documents, Monographs, Articles, Advertisements-Secondary Sources

"Adams County: Deeds for Gettysburg." *Gettysburg Compiler, January 23, 1900.* Print. *Gettysburgtimes.com.* Web 27 April 2011.

"Church History: View of the Minutes-1777-78." Gettysburg Presbyterian Church. nd. Web. 30 May 2011.

Deaths." *Adams Centinel.* 22 March 1815. *Courtesy of* ACHS.

"Died." *Adams Centinel.* 21 March 1827. Print. *Gettysburgtimes.com.* Web. 30 May 2011.

"Died-" *Republican Compiler.* 14 July 1824. 3. Print. *Gettysburgtimes. com.* Web. 30 May 2011.

"Died." *Republican Compiler.* 24 November 1824. 3. Print. *Gettysburgtimes.com.* Web. 31 May 2011.

"Editorial Response." Gettysburg Gazette, June 17, 1803. 3. Print. Gettysburgtimes.com. Web. 19 April 2011.

Davis, Edward. Advertisement. *Centinel.* 20 June 1804. Print. Courtesy of the Adams County Historical Society. Gettysburg File.

Gettys, James. Advertisement. *Centinel February 13, 1805.* Adams County Historical Society. Gettys File.

Gettys, James qtd. in Advertisement. *Gettysburg Gazette, May 27, 1803.* Print. *Gettysburgtimes.com.* Web 18 April 2011.

"Gettysburg, April 19." *Adams Centinel,* 19 April 1815. *Courtesy of* Adams County Historical Society. Gettys File..

"Gettysburg, March 15." *Adams Centinel,* 15 March 1815. *Courtesy of* Adams County Historical Society. Gettys File..

Gettysburg Presbyterian Church. "Tour of Black's Graveyard." *Gettysburg Presbyterian Church Grapevine [Newsletter].* Gettysburg: GPC, 20 May 2009. Print. Web. 12 June 2011.

"James Gettys." Advertisement. *Carlisle Gazette October 3, 1787.* Adams County Historical Society. Gettys File.

Long, Williams J. Misc. Notes. Gettysburg Lots. Adams County Historical Society. Gettysburg: ACHS, 1974.

McClean, William Archibald, Ed. *Compiler Scrapbook.* Gettysburg: Compiler, 1908. *Courtesy of* Adams County Historical Society. Gettys File.

Miscellaneous purchase receipts of Samuel Gettys and Williams McPherson. c. 1786-7. Gettys File. *Courtesy of* ACHS.

"Pennsylvania Herald and York General Advertiser: Sept 2 1789." *Abstracts of South Central Pennsylvania newspapers 1785-1790* Westminster: Family Line, P., 1988. 118. Courtesy of ACHS.

"Turnpikes." *Gettysburg Gazette, February 10, 1881.* Print. *Gettysburgtimes.com.* Web 19 April 2011.

Wright, F. Edward, Comp. "York Recorder: Nov. 4 1800." *Abstracts of South Central Pennsylvania Newspapers 1796-1800.* Westminster: Family Line P., 1988. 122. Courtesy of ACHS.

York County Heritage Trust. *York County Heritage Trust Grant Voader Mill Collection.* n.d. Web. 29 January 2011.

Printed in the United States
By Bookmasters